AF266845

Systematic Theology Guide and Workbook for Kids

A Complete Kid-Friendly Bible Study and Introduction to Christian Doctrine with Easy Lessons and Activities for Ages 7–12

TABLE OF CONTENTS

PART 2: SYSTEMATIC THEOLOGY WORKBOOK FOR KIDS

PART 1: SYSTEMATIC THEOLOGY FOR KIDS

What the Bible Says About God, Jesus, Sin, and Salvation—Explained Simply for Children

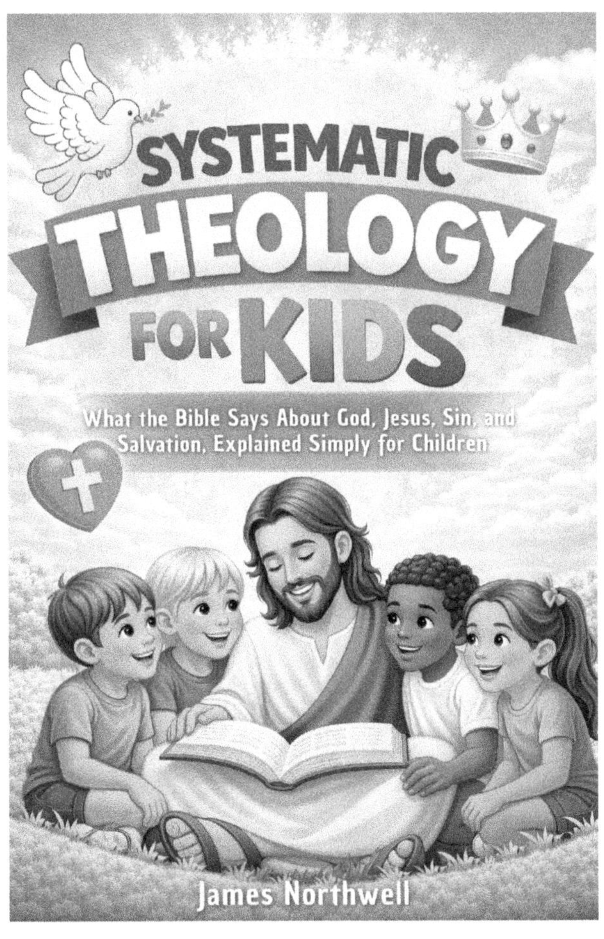

INTRODUCTION

START YOUR SEARCH FOR TRUTH

You stand on the starting line. Your heart beats fast. You want to win the game. You want to play your best. But you cannot just run onto the field without a plan. Every great athlete spends hours studying the playbook. They know the rules. They know where their teammates will be. They know what the coach expects. If you want to succeed in your sport, you have to know the facts. The same is true for your life with God. You need to know the truth about who he is and how he wants you to live.

Do you know what makes a great athlete? Discipline and knowledge are the keys to success. You do not just guess how to throw a ball or run a play. You learn the right way to do it. This book is like your spiritual playbook. It helps you organize what the Bible says so you can live with confidence. Some people think the Bible is just a collection of old stories. It does have many stories, but they all fit together into one big message. That message is what we call theology.

What Is This Big Word?

The word "theology" sounds like something for people in long robes. It sounds like something for people who spend all day in a library. But theology is actually very simple. The first part, "theo," means God. The second part, "logy," means the study of something. So, theology is just the study of God. Systematic theology is a way to organize that study. It is like a gear bag for your mind. You do not just throw your cleats, your jersey, and your water bottle into a messy pile. You put them in specific spots so you can find them when the game starts.

When we look at the Bible systematically, we put topics together. We look at everything the Bible says about God the Father in one place. Then we look at everything it says about Jesus. We do this with sin and salvation too. This helps us see the big picture. It stops us from getting confused. If you only look at one verse here and one verse there, you might miss the point. But when you see how everything fits together, the truth becomes clear. This book helps you build a solid foundation.

Why Truth Matters

You live in a world with a lot of noise. People have many different opinions about God. Some people say he is just a feeling. Others say he is a judge who waits for you to fail. Some say he does not exist at all. If you do not know the truth, you will get tossed around like a ball in a windstorm. You need to know what is real. In sports, the rules do not change based on how you feel. A foul is a foul, whether you like it or not. The truth about God is the same way. It is steady and firm.

Why do we need to organize our thoughts about God? We do this because the Bible is big and we want to see how the pieces fit together. When you understand the truth, it changes how you play. It changes how you treat your teammates. It changes how you act when you lose a game. Knowing God gives you a reason to play that is bigger than a trophy. It gives you a purpose that lasts longer than a season. You are not just playing for yourself. You are playing for the one who created you.

The Four Main Sections

We have broken this search for truth into four sections. Each one focuses on a big part of the Bible.

- **Section 1: Know Your Holy Creator.** Everything starts with God. Before there were stars or oceans or soccer fields, there was God. We will look at who he is and why we can trust his Word.
- **Section 2: Follow the Living Savior.** This section is all about Jesus. He is the hero of the story. We will see why he came to earth and what he did for us.
- **Section 3: Face the Problem of Sin.** This is the tough part of the playbook. We have to talk about what went wrong. Sin is like a major injury that keeps us out of the game. We need to know how serious it is.
- **Section 4: Join the Great Rescue.** This is the best part. It tells us how God brings us back to him. It explains how you can have a new life and a new goal.

How to Use This Playbook

You do not have to read this book all at once. You can take it one chapter at a time. Each chapter is short and direct. We use the New Standard Version (NSV) for Bible phrases. This helps keep the language clear. As you read, think about your own life. Think about your team and your school. How does the truth about God change your day?

Can a kid really understand big ideas about the Creator? Yes, because God made the truth plain enough for everyone to see. You do not need to be an adult to know the Lord. You just need to be willing to listen. God wants you to find him. He is not hiding. He has given us his Word so we can know exactly who he is.

Getting Your Mind in the Game

Training your mind is just as important as training your body. You lift weights to get strong. You run sprints to get fast. Reading this book is training for your soul. It builds your faith so you can stand strong when life gets hard. When you know the truth, you have a solid place to stand. You will not be tricked by lies. You will know your Coach, and you will know the plan.

The Bible says that the truth will set you free. That means you do not have to worry about being "good enough" on your own. You do not have to guess what God wants. He has already told us. Your job is to study the playbook and get ready to move. This is the most important search you will ever go on. It is not about finding a hidden treasure. It is about knowing the person who made the treasure in the first place.

The Goal of Our Study

The goal is not just to know facts. If you know all the rules of baseball but never pick up a bat, you are not a player. You are just a fan. We do not want to be fans of God. We want to be his followers. We want to be on his team. This study should lead you to love God more. It should make you want to talk to him in prayer. It should make you want to help others.

True theology leads to a life of action. It makes you a better friend. It makes you a harder worker. When you see how much God loves you, you cannot stay the same. You want to give him your best effort in everything you do. Whether you are on the court, in the classroom, or at home, you are representing the King.

Ready to Start?

You have your gear. You have the playbook. The field is ready. It is time to start the search. We begin with the most important person in the universe. We begin with the one who started it all. Let's look at the God who was there before time began. He is your Creator, your King, and your Father.

Psst: Don't forget to check out the Extra Content Sections at the end of this book!

SECTION ONE

KNOW YOUR HOLY CREATOR

Every team starts with a founder. Before the first whistle ever blew, someone had to build the stadium. Someone had to write the rulebook and pick the colors for the jerseys. In your life, that founder is God. This first part focuses on the Creator who started it all. You cannot know the purpose of the game if you do not know the one who created it. We start here because God is the foundation for everything else. He is the one who gives you breath to run and the strength to compete.

In these chapters, we will look at who God is. We will see that he has always been here and always will be. We will see how he talks to us through his own book. We will even look at the Father, Son, and Spirit. Finally, we will learn why we can trust him even when the score does not look good. Knowing God is the first step in your training. It gives you a reason to play with your whole heart. Get ready to meet the one who made the stars and the one who made you.

CHAPTER 1

MEET THE GOD WHO LIVES FOREVER

You know that feeling when you step onto a fresh field? The grass is cut. The lines are painted. Everything looks ready. But have you ever stopped to think about who made the dirt under your cleats? Or who made the air you breathe while you sprint? We usually focus on the game right in front of us. We worry about the next play or the halftime score. But there is a much bigger story going on. It starts with a God who does not have a "start" button.

He Has No Birthday

Everything you own has a beginning. Your favorite basketball came out of a box. Your bike was put together in a shop. Even you have a birthday that your family celebrates every year. But God is different. He is the only one who was never born. He never had a first day of school. He never had a "rookie season." He has simply always been.

The Bible uses a specific phrase for this. It says God is the "Alpha and the Omega." In the old Greek language, Alpha was the first letter of the alphabet and Omega was the last. It is like saying God is the A and the Z. He covers every single thing from the very start to the very end. He lives outside of time. While we measure our days by clocks and calendars, God just *is*.

The Coach Who Never Quits

Think about the toughest coach you know. That coach might stay late at the gym or get up early to watch film. But eventually, even the best coach has to go home and sleep. They get tired. Their voices get scratchy. They grow old and eventually stop coaching.

God never gets tired. He never needs a nap. He does not drink coffee to stay awake. The Bible says that he never slumbers or sleeps. This is a huge deal for you. It means that when you pray at three in the morning, he is listening. When you are nervous before a big 6:00 AM game, he is already awake and with you. His energy levels are always at 100 percent. He is the only one in the universe who does not need to recharge.

He Is the "I AM"

One time, a man named Moses asked God what his name was. He wanted to know what to call the person who was talking to him from a burning bush. God didn't give him a long list of titles or a fancy nickname. He just said, "I AM WHO I AM."

That sounds a bit strange at first, right? But it is actually very cool. It means God does not depend on anyone else to exist. He doesn't need a battery. He doesn't need to eat food to stay alive. He is the source of all life. Everything else in the world, the trees, the dogs, the oceans, and your teammates, needs God to keep going. But God doesn't need anything. He is perfectly happy and strong all by himself.

Seeing the Whole Field

In sports, we call it "vision." A great quarterback can see the whole field. They know where the defenders are and where their receivers are going. But even the best player can only see what is happening *right now*. They cannot see what will happen in the third quarter while they are still in the first.

God has perfect vision, but not just for space. He has perfect vision for time. He sees your past, your present, and your future all at once. He knows what the score will be before the game even starts. He knows where you will be ten years from now. Because he is eternal, he is already there. This should take a lot of pressure off your shoulders. You do not have to worry about the future because your Coach is already in the future waiting for you.

Why This Matters on the Sidelines

Why do we need to know that God lives forever? Because it makes him a "Rock." If you try to build a house on sand, it will wash away when the rain hits. If you build your life on things that change, like how many points you score or how many friends you have, you will eventually feel let down. Friends move away. Stats go down. Trophies get dusty in the attic.

God never changes. He is the same yesterday, today, and forever. His love for you today is just as strong as it was when he made the world. It will be just as strong when you are ninety years old. When everything else in your life feels like it is shifting or moving, you can hold onto God. He is the only thing in the universe that is truly permanent.

Join the Winning Team

Following an eternal God means you are on a team that can never truly lose. Even when things look bad on the scoreboard of life, we know how the story ends. God wins. He has already told us that he is the King of ages. He invites you to be part of his kingdom. This isn't a team that will fold or go out of business. It is a kingdom that lasts forever.

When you play for God, you are playing for a reward that never fades. Most athletes play for a plastic trophy or a cheap medal. Those are fun for a day, but they don't last. God offers you a life with him that goes on forever. That is the ultimate championship.

The Never-Ending Story

Most books have a final page. Most seasons have a final game. But your life with God does not have a "Game Over" screen. Because he is eternal, he can give you eternal life. This doesn't just mean you live a long time. It means you get to know the most amazing person in the universe forever.

So, next time you are running a lap or sitting on the bench, remember the God who lives forever. He was there when the first mountain was formed. He is here right now while you are reading this. And he will be there in a million years. He is the Alpha and the Omega. He is your Creator, and he is ready for the next play.

Your Daily Training

How do you act when you know God is eternal?

- **Be Patient:** If God isn't in a hurry, you don't have to be either. Trust his timing for your life.
- **Be Bold:** You are on the side of the King who never loses. You don't have to be afraid of what people think.
- **Be Thankful:** Every breath you take is a gift from the one who holds time in his hands.

God is not just a character from an old book. He is the living, breathing, eternal King. He wants you to know him today. Not just as a set of facts, but as your Coach and your Father. The race is long, but you aren't running it alone. The one who started the race is running right beside you.

CHAPTER 2

READ GOD'S OWN BOOK

Imagine you just joined a new sports team. You walk into the locker room and see a thick binder sitting on your bench. Your name is written on the front in big letters. Inside, you find everything you need to know to succeed. It has the plays for the next game. It has a list of the best foods to eat for energy. It even has a personal letter from the head coach explaining how much he believes in you. The Bible is like that binder, but it is much more important. It is the specific message that the Creator of the universe sent directly to you.

God Speaks to Us

We cannot know what God thinks just by looking at the clouds or the trees. We can see that he is smart and strong by looking at nature. However, nature does not tell us how God feels about us. It does not tell us how he wants us to live. To know those things, God had to speak. He chose to use human language so we could understand him clearly.

The Bible is not just a book filled with good advice from smart people. It is the actual Word of God. The writers were real men like David, Moses, and Peter. They used their own styles and backgrounds to write. Yet, God guided their minds so perfectly that every word they wrote was exactly what he wanted to say. A famous verse in the Bible says that all scripture is breathed out by God. This means the words came from his own breath. When you read the Bible, you are listening to God talk.

The Ultimate Scout Report

In sports, a scout report tells you the truth about your opponent and your own team. It helps you prepare for what is coming. The Bible acts as the ultimate scout report for your life. It tells you the truth about the world around you. It shows you where the traps are located. It also shows you the path to victory.

You can trust this report because God cannot lie. People make mistakes all the time. Scientists change their minds when they find new facts. Even your favorite sports analysts get their predictions wrong. God knows everything from the beginning to the end. His Word never needs an update. It is just as true today as it was thousands of years ago. You can build your whole life on these pages without worrying that the rules will change tomorrow.

One Big Story

The Bible looks like one big book, but it is actually a collection of sixty-six smaller books. These were written over a period of about 1,500 years by about forty different people. Some were kings, while others were fishermen or shepherds. You might think a book like that would be a mess. If forty different people tried to write one story over a thousand years, it would usually be full of contradictions.

Instead, the Bible tells one perfectly linked story. From the first page to the last, it points to the same plan. It shows how God created us, how we turned away, and how he sent a Savior to bring us back. This unity is a miracle. It proves that there was one main Author behind all those different writers. God was the Master Coach directing every person to play their part in the narrative.

Why You Need the Playbook

A playbook is useless if it stays in your bag during the game. You have to study it until you know the moves by heart. The same is true for the Bible. We read it so we can know God better. We do not read it just to win arguments or look smart in Sunday school. We read it to hear the voice of our Father.

The Bible is like a lamp that shows you where to step when the world feels dark. It gives you wisdom when you have to make a tough choice at school. It gives you comfort when you lose a big game or feel lonely. Most importantly, it tells you how to be saved. It is the only book in the world that can show you the way to eternal life.

How to Use Your Equipment

You probably have a routine for your sport. You stretch, you warm up, and you practice your drills. You should have a routine for reading God's Word too. Try to read a small part of it every single day. Do not feel like you have to read ten chapters at once. Even a few verses can give you something to think about while you run your laps.

Ask God to help you understand what you are reading. Since he is the Author, he is the best person to explain it to you. Look for what the text says about God first. Ask yourself what it teaches you about his character. Then, look for how you can apply it to your own life. Are there any commands to obey? Are there any promises to trust?

It Is More Than Ink and Paper

The Bible is a living book. This means it has the strength to change the way you think and act. It can reach into your heart and show you things about yourself that nobody else sees. Sometimes it might make you feel uncomfortable because it points out where you are going wrong. Other times it will fill you with more joy than a championship win.

Every time you open the Bible, you are meeting with the King. He wants to coach you through every situation you face. He wants to encourage you when you are tired. He wants to give you a goal that is bigger than any trophy. Do not let this book gather dust on your shelf. Pick it up and see what the Coach has to say to you today.

Staying in the Game

There will be times when reading the Bible feels hard. You might find parts that are confusing or names that are difficult to say. Do not give up when that happens. Just like a hard workout, the effort is worth the result. The more you read, the more the pieces will start to fit together. You will start to see the beauty of God's plan in every chapter.

Your Bible is the most valuable piece of equipment you will ever own. It is a gift from a God who loves you enough to tell you the truth. Treat it with respect and study it with excitement. The words on these pages are the very words of life. They will keep you on the right track until you reach the finish line.

CHAPTER 3

LOOK AT THE FATHER, SON, AND SPIRIT

Getting to know God can feel like trying to understand a very deep team strategy. You see different people on the field doing various jobs, but they all belong to the same organization. The Bible shows us a special truth about God that we call the Trinity. While that specific word is not in the Bible, the idea shows up on almost every single page. We believe in one God who exists as three distinct persons. These are the Father, the Son, and the Holy Spirit.

One Team and One God

The most important thing to keep in mind is that there is only one God. Christians do not worship three separate gods. That would be like saying a team has three different head coaches who never talk or agree. The Bible says clearly that the Lord is one. However, this one God is never lonely. He has always lived in a perfect relationship within himself.

Think about a triangle for a moment. A triangle is one single shape. Yet, it has three distinct corners. If you take away one corner, the triangle is gone. Each corner is part of the same one thing. This is a small way to picture how the Father, the Son, and the Spirit are all the same one God. They are equal in power and have lived forever.

The Work of the Father

We often think of God the Father as the creator and the one who holds the big plan. He is the person who sent his Son into the world because his love for us is so huge. The Father provides what we need and listens when we pray. He acts like the owner of the team who provides the stadium, the uniforms, and the chance to play. He watches over everything with a kind and steady eye.

The Father is perfectly holy and fair. You can trust him to keep his word because he has the power to make things happen. He is the source of every good thing we enjoy. When we call him our Father, we are talking about a relationship where we are safe. We are cared for by the strongest person in the universe.

The Work of the Son

Jesus Christ is the Son of God. He is not a separate god. He is the Word of God who became a human being. He came to earth to show us exactly what the Father is like. If you want to know how God feels about people who are hurting or lost, you just have to look at Jesus. He is the person of the Trinity who stepped onto the field to play the game for us.

Jesus lived a perfect life that we could never achieve on our own. He followed every rule in the Bible without making a single error. Then he took the penalty for our mistakes so we could join God's family. He is our Captain and our Savior. He is the hero who won the ultimate victory over death. Even though he is back in heaven now, he remains fully God and fully man.

The Work of the Spirit

The Holy Spirit is often the person of the Trinity that kids find the most mysterious. He does not have a physical body like Jesus did, but he is just as much God as the Father and the Son. The Spirit is like the internal drive and wisdom that helps an athlete perform at their peak. He lives inside every person who follows Jesus.

The Holy Spirit helps us understand the Bible when we read it. He gives us the strength to say no to things that are wrong. He also comforts us when we feel sad or afraid. Think of him as the Coach who is always with you on the sidelines. He whispers the truth to your heart and reminds you of what Jesus taught. He is the one who changes us from the inside out so we can look more like our Captain every day.

Working Together for You

The Father, the Son, and the Spirit always work together in perfect harmony. They never argue about what to do next. They never have different goals. When God created the world, all three persons were there. When Jesus was baptized in the river, the Father spoke from heaven and the Spirit came down like a dove. They are the perfect team.

This matters for your life because it shows that God is a God of love. Before anything else was made, the Father, Son, and Spirit loved each other. Because God is a relationship, he made you for a relationship too. He wants you to know the Father, follow the Son, and listen to the Spirit. You are invited to join in the life of God.

Why This Knowledge Is a Huge Advantage

Knowing about the Trinity helps you see how big and amazing God really is. He is much more than just a powerful man in the sky. He is a beautiful being who is far beyond what we can imagine. This should make us feel a sense of wonder. We serve a King who is so great that we cannot even fully explain him with simple words.

When you are out on the field, remember that you are never alone. The Father is watching over you as your provider. The Son is leading you as your Captain. The Holy Spirit is inside you giving you the power to act with courage. You have the whole team of heaven on your side. That kind of support gives you a confidence that no opponent can ever shake.

Training Your Heart

You might not understand everything about the Trinity today. That is perfectly fine. Even the smartest adults still find it hard to explain. The goal is not to solve a math puzzle but to know a person. Spend time talking to each person of the Trinity. Thank the Father for making you. Thank the Son for saving you. Ask the Holy Spirit to guide your steps at school and during your games.

As you grow, you will see the fingerprints of the Father, Son, and Spirit all over your life. You will see how they work together to lead you toward the finish line. You belong to a God who is one, yet three. He is your Creator, your Savior, and your Comforter. Stay close to him and watch how he uses his power to help you grow into the athlete and person he wants you to be.

CHAPTER 4

TRUST THE GOD WHO RULES EVERYTHING

Think about a game where the referee has lost total control of the field. Players are breaking rules left and right, the scoreboard is blinking random numbers, and nobody knows which way to run. It would be impossible to play your best in a mess like that. Thankfully, the universe is not a chaotic mess. God is in total control of every single thing that happens. We call this his sovereignty. It means he is the ultimate King who rules over the stars, the shifting weather, and even the final score of your game.

The King on the Throne

God does not just watch the world go by like a fan sitting in the back of the bleachers. He is the one running the entire show from start to finish. He has the authority to do whatever he pleases, and his plans never fail. The Bible says that our God is in the heavens and he does all that he purposed. Not a single sparrow falls to the ground without him knowing about it. If he cares about the life of a tiny bird, you can be sure he cares about every small detail of your day.

This can be hard to wrap our minds around when things go wrong. We might wonder why God allows a rainout on the day of a big tournament or why he lets a teammate get injured. We have to remember that God sees the whole map while we only see the next turn in the road. He is like a master coach who sees the end of the long season from the very first day of summer practice. He uses even the tough times to build our character and lead us toward his good goals. He is never surprised by a bad bounce or a late goal.

No Accidents in the Plan

Sometimes we use the word luck. We say someone got a lucky bounce or a lucky break at the buzzer. In reality, there is no such thing as luck when you follow the King of the universe. Every "bounce" in life is under his watch. This does not mean we should be lazy and stop practicing our drills. God wants us to work hard and give our best effort in everything we do. But we can rest at night knowing that the results are always in his hands.

Knowing that God rules everything takes the heavy pressure off your shoulders. You do not have to carry the weight of the whole world. You just have to be faithful to your part of the plan. If you win the championship, you can thank him for the victory. If you lose the game, you can trust that he has a reason for that outcome too. He is working all things together for the good of those who love him. He is the one who decides when the sun rises and when the rain falls.

Freedom from the Weight of Worry

Worry is like trying to run laps while wearing a heavy backpack filled with rocks. It slows you down and makes you tired before the game even starts. Most of our worry comes from trying to control things we cannot change. We worry about what other people think or what might happen at school tomorrow. But when you realize that God is the one in charge, you can drop that backpack on the ground.

The Bible tells us not to be anxious about anything. We can trade our worry for prayer because we know the King is our Father. He has the power to provide for you and the wisdom to lead you through the dark. Since he is already in control of tomorrow, you can focus on doing your best today. You are safe in the hands of the one who commands the wind and the waves with a single word. He is never overwhelmed by the problems we face.

Trusting the Process of Training

In sports, you have to trust the process. You might not see why a coach makes you do a certain boring drill until months later when you are in the middle of a game. Trusting God is very similar to that. His ways are much higher than our ways. We might think we know the best path to take, but he knows the perfect path that leads to growth.

There will be days when the "play" God has called for your life does not make sense to you. Those are the moments when your trust is tested. Remind yourself of who is in charge of the universe. He is the God who lives forever. He is the God who wrote the Book you read. He is the Father, the Son, and the Holy Spirit. Because he is all of those things, he is worthy of your total trust even when the score looks bad.

A Peace That Stays with You

When you truly believe that God rules everything, you gain a special kind of peace. It is a quiet confidence that stays with you even when the stadium is loud or the pressure is high. This peace does not come from your own skills or your own strength. It comes from knowing that your King is sitting on his throne and he loves you.

This does not mean life will always be easy or that you will win every trophy. It means that even when life is hard, you are never alone on the field. Your Coach is not surprised by the challenges you face. He is using every circumstance to make you stronger and to show his glory to the world. Stand firm in that truth. The God who rules the vast universe is the same God who calls you his own child. He has the final say in all things, and his kingdom will never end.

Resting in His Power

At the end of a long day, you can lay your head down and sleep because God is awake. He does not need to rest, so you can. You do not have to stay up wondering if the world will fall apart. He is holding the stars in place and keeping your heart beating. His sovereignty is like a soft pillow for a tired athlete.

When you wake up, remember that you are walking into a day that God has already planned. Whether you face a big test, a hard practice, or a fun day with friends, he is in charge. He has given you exactly what you need for the tasks ahead. Trust his power, rely on his wisdom, and play your heart out for the King who rules everything.

SECTION TWO

FOLLOW THE LIVING SAVIOR

Every team needs that one star player who can step up and change the whole game. You know the type. When the score is down, the crowd is quiet, and the clock is ticking toward zero, you look for the person who can carry the weight of the team. In the history of the whole world, that person is Jesus Christ. This second part is all about the Savior who stepped out of heaven and onto our messy field. We call him the living Savior because he is not just a name in an old history book or a statue in a building. He is alive right now.

In the next four chapters, we are going to follow the path of Jesus from his humble start in a barn to his massive victory over the grave. We will see why he is the hero the world was waiting for since the very beginning. We will watch how he played the game of life without breaking a single rule. Then, we will look at the most important moment in all of history: his sacrifice on the cross and his return to life. Understanding Jesus is the key to understanding everything else in your life. He is the Captain of our faith and the only one who can lead us across the finish line.

CHAPTER 1

SEE THE PROMISED HERO ARRIVE

If you have ever sat by your phone waiting for a massive trade or a new superstar to join your team, you know that waiting is the hardest part. You check the news every five minutes. You imagine how much the team will change once the big name finally shows up. For thousands of years, the people in the Bible were stuck in that same waiting room. They were looking for a Hero. God promised a Savior right after the very first sin happened in the garden. He told his people that a King was coming to crush the power of evil and set them free for good.

A Very Strange Entrance

When a famous athlete arrives in a new city, you usually see flashing lights and expensive cars. You see big crowds and fancy hotels. But when the King of the entire universe arrived on earth, he did not come with a parade. He did not check into a mansion or move into a palace. Instead, Jesus was born in a quiet, dusty town called Bethlehem. His first bed was a manger. That is just a wooden box where people put hay for cows and sheep to eat.

This tells you something huge about your Hero. Jesus did not come to show off or act like he was too good for us. He came to be near us. He became a real human being with skin and bones. He felt the cold. He got hungry. He had to learn how to walk just like you did. The Bible calls him Immanuel. That name means "God with us." He stepped off his throne and entered our world to play on our level.

Checking the Scouting Reports

Long before Jesus took his first breath, God gave his people scouting reports called prophecies. These were specific clues written down by prophets hundreds of years before the birth of Christ. They told the people exactly where the Savior would be born and what his family tree would look like.

- The reports said he would be born in the small town of Bethlehem.
- They said he would come from the royal family of King David.
- They said his mother would be a virgin.

Jesus hit every single one of those marks. The odds of one person doing that by accident are impossible. It would be like a player predicting every single play of a game perfectly before it even started. This proves that Jesus was not just a lucky teacher. He was the one God planned to send since the world began. He was the promised Hero, and he showed up right on time.

Both God and Man

This is the most amazing part of the whole playbook. Jesus is 100 percent God and 100 percent man at the same time. It is a mystery that is hard to explain, but it is why he is the only one who can save us. Because he is a man, he can represent you. He knows what it feels like to be tempted or to feel sad. He knows what it is like to have sore muscles after a long day of work.

Because he is God, he has the power to fix what is broken. He has the authority to forgive every bad choice you have ever made. He has the strength to defeat death itself. Think of it like a coach who was once a world-class player. He knows the struggle because he played the game, but he has the master plan to lead the team to a win. Jesus is the bridge between heaven and earth.

The Mission of the Hero

Why did the Hero come? He did not show up just to do cool miracles or give long speeches. He came on a rescue mission. The world was stuck on a losing streak because of sin. We were separated from God and could not find the way back home on our own. Jesus arrived to be our substitute. He came to live the life we should have lived and to take the penalty we deserved.

His arrival was the start of the greatest comeback story in history. From the moment he breathed in the air of that stable, he was heading toward a goal. He was focused on the work of his Father. He was here to win back what was lost and to invite you onto his winning team. The Hero has arrived, and the world will never be the same again.

CHAPTER 2

WATCH JESUS LIVE A PERFECT LIFE

Imagine a player who goes through an entire career without ever making a single mistake. This player never misses a shot, never drops a pass, and never commits a foul. In the world of sports, that is basically impossible. Even the greatest legends have bad days or make poor choices when the pressure is high. But when Jesus stepped onto the earth, he did something no one else has ever done. He lived a life of total perfection. He followed every single rule of God with a perfect heart and perfect actions every single second of his life.

The Training Ground of Nazareth

Jesus did not start his public work until he was about thirty years old. Before he was a famous teacher, he was a child and a young man living in a humble town called Nazareth. He grew up in a regular home and worked with his hands as a carpenter. This part of his life is very important for us to see. It shows that he understands what it is like to be a kid and a teenager. He knows what it feels like to have chores to do and lessons to learn.

The Bible tells us that Jesus grew in wisdom and in stature. He also grew in favor with God and man. He had to learn his lessons at school and obey his parents at home. Even as a boy, he was focused on his Father's business. He lived a quiet life of obedience, preparing for the big mission ahead. He was training in the small things so that he would be ready for the big things. Think of this as the long years of practice that nobody sees before the championship game. Jesus was faithful in the workshop and in the home long before he was famous.

Facing the Ultimate Opponent

Before Jesus started his ministry, he went into the wilderness for forty days. While he was there, he was tempted by the devil. This was like a championship match between good and evil with the highest stakes imaginable. The devil tried to get Jesus to cheat, to show off, and to take the easy way out. He used every trick in the book to try and make Jesus stumble or doubt who he was.

Jesus did not give in for even a second. Every time the devil tempted him, Jesus fought back with the Word of God. He quoted scripture to keep his mind focused on the truth. Because he stayed strong, he proved that he was the perfect Hero. He succeeded where everyone else had failed. He showed that he had the discipline and the power to overcome any temptation that comes our way. When you feel tempted to cheat or quit, remember that your Captain has already beaten that opponent.

Playing for the Father's Glory

When Jesus began traveling and teaching, people were amazed by him. He healed the sick, made the blind see, and even walked on water during a storm. He had all the power in the world, yet he never once used it for himself. He did not try to become a rich king or a famous celebrity. Every miracle he performed was done to show people who God is and to help those who were hurting.

Jesus always did exactly what the Father told him to do. He said that his food was to do the will of the one who sent him. He lived with a single goal: to honor God. Whether he was talking to a huge crowd on a mountain or sitting quietly with a friend, his heart was always in the right place. He loved people perfectly, even when they were mean to him. He spoke the truth perfectly, even when it was hard to hear. He was never "faking it" for the cameras. He was the real deal.

Our Perfect Representative

Why did Jesus have to be perfect? Why couldn't he just be a "mostly good" person like us? The answer is found in the rules of the game. God is perfectly holy, and we are not. Because of our sin, we are disqualified from being in God's presence. We needed someone to play the game in our place. We needed a substitute who could turn in a perfect scorecard.

Jesus lived that life for you. When God looks at those who follow Jesus, he does not see our mistakes and our fouls. He sees the perfect record of his Son. Jesus earned the "win" that we could never earn on our own. He is like a captain who scores all the points for a team that was losing. Because he was perfect, he was the only one who could eventually pay the price for our sins. If he had sinned even once, he could not have saved us.

Learning from the Master

Watching Jesus live his life gives us the best example of how we should live. He showed us how to be brave when people are being bullies. He showed us how to be kind to people that everyone else ignores. He showed us that true greatness comes from serving others rather than trying to be the most important person in the room. He washed the feet of his disciples, showing that no job is too small for a leader.

When you are at school or on the field, you can ask yourself how Jesus would handle the situation. How would he treat a teammate who made a mistake? How would he act when a referee makes a bad call? While we will never be perfect like he is, we can move in the right direction by following his lead. We have the best Coach in history showing us the way. He does not just tell us what to do; he showed us how to do it.

A Life of Constant Prayer

One of the most interesting things about the perfect life of Jesus was how much he prayed. Even though he was God, he spent hours talking to his Father. He would often get up very early in the morning or go up on a mountain alone to pray. This was the secret to his strength. He stayed connected to the source of his power every single day.

This teaches us that even the strongest person needs to rely on God. If Jesus needed to pray to live a godly life, how much more do we need to pray? He shows us that a perfect life is a life of dependence. It is not about being "tough" enough to do it alone. It is about staying close to the Father and listening to his voice. Prayer was the "huddle" where Jesus got his instructions.

The Finish Line in Sight

Jesus lived every day knowing that a very difficult day was coming. He knew his perfect life would eventually lead him to the cross. He did not run away from that destiny or try to hide. He stayed the course with courage and love. His perfection was not just for show; it was part of the rescue plan. He was the perfect Lamb of God who was preparing to give his life for his friends.

As you follow Jesus through the pages of the Bible, pay attention to the small details. Notice his kindness to children, his honesty with leaders, and his total obedience to his Father. There has never been anyone like him, and there never will be again. He is the living Savior who lived the perfect life so that we could have a renewed life in him. His victory is now our victory.

Consistency Under Pressure

Think about the times you have felt the most pressure. Maybe it was a final exam or the last minute of a tie game. It is easy to be "good" when things are easy, but it is hard when things get tough. Jesus was perfect even when people were shouting at him and trying to trap him. He never lost his temper in a sinful way. He never lied to protect himself.

His consistency is what makes him so trustworthy. You never have to wonder which "version" of Jesus you are going to get. He is the same yesterday, today, and forever. His perfect life is a solid rock you can stand on when your own life feels shaky. When you feel like a failure, you can look at his success and remember that he is on your team.

The Power of His Words

Jesus did not just act perfectly; he spoke perfectly too. He said things that changed the world forever. He taught us to love our enemies and to pray for those who treat us badly. He told stories that helped us understand God's love in a new way. Even the people who didn't like him had to admit that nobody ever spoke like he did.

Every word that came out of his mouth was filled with truth and grace. He never used his words to tear people down just to make himself look big. He used his words to heal, to teach, and to lead. This is another area where we can watch him and learn. If we want to be like our

Captain, we need to watch how we speak to our teammates, our teachers, and our families.

Final Thoughts on a Perfect Life

The perfect life of Jesus is the foundation of our faith. Without it, we would have no hope of being right with God. He did the hard work of obeying every command so that we could enjoy the blessing of being called God's children. It is a gift we could never buy and a trophy we could never win on our own.

As you go through your week, try to keep your eyes on the Master. Study his moves in the Bible. Listen to his coaching through the Holy Spirit. Remember that you are following the only person who ever played the game perfectly. He is not just a model to follow; he is the Savior who holds you up when you fall.

CHAPTER 3

STAND NEAR THE CROSS

In every great sports movie, there is a moment where it looks like the hero has lost. The star player is down on the turf, the lights are dimming, and the opposing team is celebrating. To anyone watching, the game is over. Standing near the cross of Jesus feels like that moment. It is the darkest part of the story. If you were there that day, you would have seen a crowd mocking a man who was dying. You would have seen his friends running away in fear. It looked like a total defeat. But in reality, this was the most important victory in the history of the universe. This was the moment the "Promised Hero" finished his biggest mission.

The Most Difficult Play

We have talked about how Jesus lived a perfect life. He never committed a foul. He never broke a rule. Because of that, he was the only person who did not deserve to die. Death is the penalty for sin, and since Jesus had no sin, death had no claim on him. Yet, he chose to go to the cross anyway. He did not go because he was caught or because he was weak. He went because it was the only way to save us.

Think of it like a teammate taking a massive hit so that you can score the winning goal. Jesus took the "hit" for every bad thing we have ever done. All of our lies, our anger, and our selfishness were placed on his shoulders. The Bible says that he became sin for us. While he hung on that cross, he was paying a debt that he did not owe because we owed a debt we could never pay. It was the most difficult "play" ever called, and Jesus ran it perfectly.

The Weight of the World

When Jesus was in the garden the night before he died, he was in deep agony. He knew what was coming. He wasn't just afraid of the physical pain, although the cross was a terrible way to die. He was feeling the weight of the Father's justice against sin. Throughout his whole life, Jesus had been in perfect, happy fellowship with God the Father. On the cross, that was going to change.

As Jesus hung there, the sky went pitch black in the middle of the afternoon. It was as if the sun refused to watch. Jesus cried out, asking why God had forsaken him. In that moment, he was experiencing the separation from God that we deserved. He was being shut out so that we could be let in. He was treated like an enemy so that we could be treated like friends. He carried the weight of the world's darkness so we could walk in the light.

The Words from the Cross

Even while he was in terrible pain, Jesus was still coaching us on how to love. He didn't scream threats at the people who were hurting him. Instead, he prayed for them. He asked the Father to forgive them because they didn't understand what they were doing. He also made sure his mother was cared for, showing that he never stopped being a loving son.

One of the men being executed next to Jesus realized who he was. This man was a criminal who had actually done wrong things. He asked Jesus to remember him. Jesus didn't tell him it was too late or that he needed to go back and do good deeds first. He told the man, "Today you will be with me in paradise." This shows us that the cross is for everyone. It doesn't matter how many games you have lost or how many mistakes you have made. If you turn to Jesus, his victory becomes yours.

"It Is Finished"

Right before Jesus died, he shouted out three powerful words: "It is finished!" In the original language, this was a word used by businessmen when a bill was paid in full. It was also a word a general might use when a war was won. Jesus wasn't saying, "I am finished," like a person who has given up. He was saying that the work of salvation was complete.

The "score" was settled. The sacrifice was made. There was nothing left for us to do to earn our way to God. The bridge that had been broken back in the Garden of Eden was now fixed. When Jesus died, a thick curtain in the Temple tore in half from top to bottom. This was God's way of showing that the door was wide open. Anyone could now come to him through Jesus. The game-winning play had been executed, and the clock hit zero on the power of sin.

Why the Blood Matters

You might wonder why there had to be so much pain and blood. Why couldn't God just say, "I forgive you," and leave it at that? The reason is that God is perfectly just. If a judge let a criminal go free without any punishment, that judge wouldn't be a good judge. Someone had to pay the price for the rules we broke.

The blood of Jesus is what cleans us. Just like you might use water to wash the mud off your jersey after a rainy game, the blood of Jesus washes the stain of sin off our souls. Because he was the perfect Son of God, his sacrifice was big enough to cover every person who has ever lived. He was the "Lamb of God" who took away the sin of the world. It was a high price, but he paid it because he saw you were worth it.

Standing in the Shadow of the Cross

When we stand near the cross in our minds, we see two things at the same time. We see how bad our sin is, and we see how great God's love is. Our sin must be very serious if it took the death of the Son of God to fix it. But God's love must be incredibly deep if he was willing to go through that for us.

For an athlete, the cross is the ultimate lesson in sacrifice. It shows us that true strength isn't about crushing others; it's about giving yourself for others. Jesus didn't use his power to save himself; he used his power to stay on that cross until the job was done. He showed us that the way to lead is to serve. When you feel like you have to be the best and the most famous to be important, look at the cross. The King of the world made himself nothing so that you could have everything.

The Silence of the Saturday

After Jesus died, his friends took his body down and put it in a tomb. They rolled a massive stone in front of the entrance. It was a very sad and quiet time. His followers thought they had lost. They didn't understand yet that the "defeat" of the cross was actually the secret to their victory.

Sometimes in our lives, it feels like "Saturday." It feels like God is silent and the bad guys are winning. We might feel like our prayers aren't being heard or that our mistakes are too big to fix. But we have to remember that Friday's cross happened for a reason, and Sunday is coming. The cross wasn't an accident. It was the plan. God was working even when it looked like he was losing.

A Love That Never Quits

If you ever doubt if God loves you, you only have to look at the cross. You don't have to wonder if he cares or if he is listening. He proved his love in the most dramatic way possible. He didn't just say "I love you" from a distance; he came down and bled for you. He went through the worst pain imaginable so that he would never have to be without you.

This changes the way we live. We don't follow God because we are afraid of getting in trouble. We follow him because we are amazed by what he did on that hill. We play our best because we want to honor the Captain who gave his life for the team. The cross is the place where we find our true identity. We are people who were worth dying for.

Training Your Heart at the Cross

How does standing near the cross change your daily life at school or on the team?

- **It kills pride:** You can't brag about how good you are when you realize you needed a Savior to die for you.

- **It gives courage:** If Jesus died for you, you don't have to be afraid of what people think of you.

- **It teaches forgiveness:** If God forgave you for so much, you can forgive your teammate who messed up.

The cross is the center of everything we believe. It is the moment where the Hero took our place and won the war. It looks like a tragedy, but it is actually the greatest victory ever. Take a moment to thank Jesus for staying on that cross. He did it for his Father's glory, and he did it for you.

CHAPTER 4

CELEBRATE THE KING WHO ROSE AGAIN

Think about the biggest comeback you have ever seen. Maybe your team was down by twenty points with only a few minutes left on the clock. The fans were already heading for the parking lot. The other side was laughing on the sidelines, basically celebrating a win that hadn't happened yet. It looked like the lights were about to go out on your season. Then, everything flipped. A quick score, a big defensive stop, and suddenly the momentum shifted so fast it made your head spin. You won a game that nobody thought was possible.

The resurrection of Jesus is the ultimate version of that story. It is the greatest comeback in the history of the world. It is the moment where the "losing side" walked off the field as the undisputed champions of the universe.

The Sunday Morning Surprise

On the Sunday morning after Jesus died on the cross, a few of his friends walked toward his tomb. They weren't carrying pom-poms or victory signs. They were carrying heavy spices to put on a dead body. They weren't expecting a miracle; they were expecting a funeral. They were sad, tired, and probably feeling like the last three years had been a massive waste of time. But when they rounded the corner into the garden, they saw something that stopped their hearts. The massive stone that sealed the grave had been tossed aside like a piece of trash.

An angel was sitting right there, and he didn't look like he was at a funeral. He gave them the news that changed every single thing about our world: "He is not here, for he has risen." That one sentence meant the grave couldn't hold him. It meant the "Game Over" screen was a lie. Jesus didn't just survive an injury. He conquered death itself. He walked out of that dark hole on his own two feet, breathing the morning air as the Champion of life.

He Is Not a Ghost

Some people try to say the resurrection was just a nice dream or a vision. But the Bible goes out of its way to show that Jesus was physically, tangibly alive. He didn't just haunt a room like a blurry ghost. He met with his friends for breakfast. He walked on the dirt roads with them. He even ate a piece of fish to prove his stomach worked. One of his followers, a guy named Thomas, wouldn't believe it until he actually touched the scars on the hands of Jesus. Jesus let him do it. He wanted his team to have 100 percent proof that their Captain was back.

At one point, more than five hundred people saw him at the same time. This wasn't a secret. It was a public victory lap. Think about how many cameras and witnesses it takes to make a world record "official." Jesus had hundreds of witnesses who saw him, talked to him, and touched him. These people were so sure he was alive that they spent the rest of their lives telling the story, even when it got them thrown in jail. You don't die for a fairy tale. You die for a King you have seen with your own eyes.

Breaking Death's Winning Streak

Why does a story from two thousand years ago matter to you today? It matters because death is the one opponent that scares everyone. Even the fastest athletes, the most powerful kings, and the smartest scientists eventually have to face the end. It is the ultimate "undefeated" rival. But when Jesus rose again, he broke death's winning streak for good. He proved that he has the keys to the grave in his pocket.

Because Jesus is alive, you don't have to live in fear. You know that this life on earth is just the pre-game. For everyone on Jesus' team, death is just a tunnel that leads to a much better stadium. It is a doorway to an eternal kingdom where there are no more injuries, no more losses, and no more pain. Jesus showed us the way through. He is the first one out of the grave, and he promises that we are going to follow him.

The Receipt for the Cross

Remember how we talked about Jesus paying for our sins on the cross? The resurrection is like the receipt for that payment. If Jesus had stayed in the grave, we would never know for sure if his sacrifice actually worked. We might wonder if God the Father actually accepted the payment. But by raising Jesus from the dead, God was putting his official stamp of approval on the whole mission.

It was God's way of saying, "The price is paid. The work is finished. The win is in the books." The resurrection proves that Jesus is exactly who he said he was. He is the Son of God and the King of kings. If he has the power to bring himself back to life, he definitely has the power to handle your life. He can handle your biggest mistakes, your deepest fears, and your entire future.

New Power for Your Daily Game

The resurrection didn't just happen so Jesus could be famous. It happened so you could have a new kind of power. The same strength that raised Jesus from the dead is now available to you through the Holy Spirit. This isn't just "positive thinking" or trying to be a better person on your own. It is real, spiritual energy that helps you live for God when things get tough.

Think about a controller for a video game. If the batteries are dead, it doesn't matter how hard you mash the buttons; the character on the screen won't move. But when you put in fresh batteries, it works perfectly. Before we know Jesus, we are like those dead batteries. We don't have the "juice" to live the way we were made to live. But because Jesus is alive, he plugs us into his own life. He gives us the strength to be kind when we want to be mean, and to be brave when we want to quit. We are living on resurrection power.

You Serve a Living King

Most famous people from history are dead and gone. You can visit their graves or read their old books, but you can't have a conversation with them. You can't ask a coach from a hundred years ago for advice on your next play. But Jesus is a living King. You can talk to him right now. He is active in the world, and he is active in your life today.

This changes the way we worship. We don't just sing songs about a hero from the past. We sing to a Friend who is actually in the room. We don't just follow a list of old rules. We follow a Leader who is calling our name. Every time you step onto the field or into a classroom, you can know that the Living King is right there with you. You are playing for an audience of One, and he is more alive than anyone else in the stands.

The Celebration That Never Ends

The resurrection is a reason to celebrate every single morning. In the early church, the followers of Jesus were so hyped about the resurrection that they moved their main meeting day to Sunday. They wanted to start every week remembering that their Captain won the war. That is why most churches meet on Sunday today. It is a weekly reminder that the tomb is empty and the King is on the throne.

As an athlete, this gives you a perspective that nobody can shake. If the worst thing that can happen to you is death, and Jesus has already beaten death, then what is there to really be afraid of? You can play with total freedom. You don't have to be perfect to be loved, because Jesus' victory is already credited to you. You can take risks, you can be humble, and you can give your all, knowing that the ultimate prize is already locked in.

Training for a New Kind of Victory

How do you live like a "resurrection person" during the week?

- **Live with Hope:** Even when you have a bad day or a tough loss, remember that the story isn't over yet. God is the expert at comebacks.
- **Talk to the King:** Since he is alive, treat him like he is real. Share your worries and your big wins with him in prayer.
- **Share the News:** Tell your teammates the good news. You have a Savior who is more powerful than a stone grave!

The resurrection is the final piece of the puzzle. Without it, the cross is just a tragedy. With it, the cross is a total victory. Jesus Christ is not just a memory; he is the Master of the universe. He has finished the work, he has won the game, and he is inviting you to share in his glory. Pick up your gear, head out to the field, and play with the joy of a champion. The tomb is empty, and the best is yet to come.

SECTION THREE

FACE THE PROBLEM OF SIN

Every legendary story has a massive conflict. To truly value the victory Jesus won, we have to look closely at why we needed a rescue mission in the first place. This third part dives into the "injury" that affected the entire human race. We call it sin. It is the core reason the world feels broken and why we often struggle to do what is right, even when we want to.

In these four chapters, we are going back to the very start of the timeline. We will see the perfect world God designed and how things went off the tracks. We will look at why sin is such a big deal and why we cannot simply practice our way out of the problem. Understanding the weight of sin is not meant to make you feel bad. It is meant to show you how much you are loved. Once you realize how deep the hole was, you will see how amazing it is that God reached all the way down to pull you out.

CHAPTER 1

START WITH A PERFECT CREATION

Before you can understand a broken bone on an X-ray, you have to know what a healthy bone looks like. To understand why the world is so messy today, we have to look back at the original blueprints. God did not create a world full of sadness, sickness, or mean teammates. In the beginning, everything was "very good." It was the ultimate home court, designed by the greatest Architect to be a place of total joy and peace.

The Masterpiece of the Universe

God did not just throw the world together like a last-minute school project. He crafted it with incredible detail and care. He spoke, and light appeared out of nothing. He carved out the deep canyons and poured the massive oceans into place. He designed every leaf, every star, and every atom. When he got to the very end of his work, he created his most important masterpiece: human beings.

The Bible says that God made us in his own image. This does not mean we look like him physically, but that we were made to reflect his character to the rest of creation. We were made to be smart, creative, and loving. Most importantly, we were made to be in a close, walking relationship with him. Imagine being on a team where the Owner is your best friend and the Head Coach is your biggest fan. That was life in the Garden of Eden. There was no fear, no shame, and no hiding.

No Fouls and No Errors

In this original world, there was no such thing as a "bad day." Adam and Eve, the first humans, lived in a place of perfect harmony. They didn't argue with each other or get their feelings hurt. They didn't feel lonely or anxious about the future. There were no injuries to worry about and no trophies to fight over because they already had everything they needed.

They had a job to do, which was to take care of the beautiful world God made. Work wasn't a tiring chore back then; it was a way to worship. They walked and talked with God in the cool of the day. There was no wall between heaven and earth. It was a world where every single play was successful and every moment was filled with purpose. You could say they were playing the game of life at the highest possible level, and they were winning every single day.

The One Specific Rule

Even though they had total freedom to enjoy the garden, God gave them one specific boundary. He told them they could eat from any tree in the garden except for one: the Tree of the Knowledge of Good and Evil. This wasn't because God was being mean or trying to hide something fun from them. It was a test of trust and loyalty.

Every real relationship needs trust and the power to choose. For Adam and Eve to truly love God, they had to have the choice to follow him or walk away. The rule was there to remind them that God was the King and they were his people. As long as they stayed within that boundary, life would stay perfect. It was a simple rule for a perfect life. It gave them the chance to show God that they valued his wisdom more than their own desires.

A Reflection of True Greatness

When you look at a beautiful sunset or see a perfectly executed play on the field, you are seeing a small "glimmer" of that original world. Deep down, we all feel like the world should be better than it is. We feel like things are "wrong" when we see people hurting or being unfair. That feeling exists because we were made for perfection. We were made for the Garden of Eden.

God's original plan shows us how much value we actually have. You aren't an accident or a random mistake. You aren't just a number on a jersey or a name on a roster. You are a high-definition image-bearer of the Living God. You were designed for greatness, for goodness, and for a friendship with your Creator that lasts forever. Starting with a perfect creation helps us see exactly what we lost when sin entered the picture. It also shows us exactly what Jesus came to win back for us in the end.

The Purpose of the Design

Everything in a sports stadium has a purpose. The lights are there so you can see. The lines are there to define the field. The whistle is there to start the action. In the same way, everything in the original creation had a reason for existing. Humans were designed to be the "captains" of the earth, leading the way in showing how great God is.

When things work according to their design, they are beautiful. When a car stays on the road, it gets you where you need to go. When an athlete follows the play, the team succeeds. Adam and Eve were perfectly "on track" with God's design. They were living in the light, and there was no shadow of doubt or sin to be found. Understanding this perfection is the only way to realize how tragic the next part of the story really is.

A World Without Shadows

In the Garden, there was no such thing as a secret. Adam and Eve were completely open with God and with each other. They didn't have to pretend to be someone else to be liked. They didn't have to perform to feel important. Their value didn't come from how fast they could run or how much they knew. It came from the fact that God made them and loved them.

This is the "gold standard" of life. It is the life we all go looking for when we try to be successful or popular. We are trying to get back to that feeling of being totally accepted and totally at peace. God started us off with that gift. He gave us a perfect start to the game. But as we will see in the next chapter, a new challenger was waiting in the shadows to try and ruin the perfect season.

CHAPTER 2

LEARN HOW SIN ENTERED THE WORLD

Every team has an opponent who plays dirty. You know the type. They wait for you to get tired, then they whisper things to get in your head. They try to make you doubt your coach or your own skills. In the perfect garden God made, an enemy showed up to do exactly that. He didn't use a physical weapon to ruin the world. He used a lie. This is the moment where the "perfect season" came to a crashing halt. It is the moment sin entered the game.

The Great Deception

The Bible introduces a character called the serpent. He was clever and sneaky. He didn't walk up to Adam and Eve and tell them to hate God. Instead, he asked a very tricky question: "Did God actually say you shall not eat of any tree in the garden?" He wanted them to focus on the one thing they couldn't have instead of the thousands of things they could.

He made it sound like God was holding out on them. He suggested that God was keeping them back from something better. The serpent told them that if they ate the fruit, they would be like God. He made them believe that they didn't need a Coach anymore. He convinced them that they could be their own bosses and make their own rules. This was the first "foul" in human history, and it changed everything.

The Choice That Broke the World

Adam and Eve listened to the lie. They looked at the fruit, they wanted it, and they took a bite. In that one moment, they stepped outside of the boundaries God had set. This was the birth of sin. Sin is not just "doing a bad thing." At its core, sin is a rebellion. It is telling God, "I know better than you do." It is like a player deciding to ignore every play the coach calls and just doing whatever they feel like on the field.

The second they ate the fruit, the world changed. The "perfect health" of creation vanished. Suddenly, they felt something they had never felt before: shame. They realized they were naked and they tried to hide from God among the trees. The friendship was broken. The light was gone. They had traded a relationship with the King for a piece of fruit, and the trade was a disaster.

The Ripple Effect

When a key player on a team gets a serious injury, it doesn't just hurt them. It affects the whole roster. It changes the way the game is played for everyone. When Adam and Eve sinned, it caused a "spiritual injury" that passed down to every human being who would ever be born. It was like a virus that got into the DNA of the human race.

Because of that one choice, everything in creation started to wear out. This is why we have sickness, why plants grow thorns, and why we have to work so hard for everything we get. The harmony was gone. Animals started to fight, and people started to argue. Sin didn't just stay in that one garden. it spread like a shadow across the entire globe. Every mistake, every war, and every tear can be traced back to this moment in the locker room of history.

The Blame Game

When God came looking for Adam and Eve, they didn't own up to what they did. Adam blamed Eve. Eve blamed the serpent. This was the very first "blame game." Instead of asking for forgiveness, they tried to point the finger at someone else. This is something we still do today. When we mess up a play or get a bad grade, our first instinct is often to blame the ref, the teacher, or our teammates.

Sin makes us want to hide the truth. It makes us want to look good on the outside even when things are messy on the inside. God saw right through their excuses. He is a holy God, and he cannot just ignore a broken rule. There had to be consequences for what happened. The perfect garden was no longer their home. They had to leave, and a massive angel was placed at the gate to keep them out. The "home court advantage" was officially lost.

The First Promise of a Comeback

The story of how sin entered the world is very sad, but it ends with a glimmer of hope. Even while God was explaining the consequences of their sin, he made a promise. He told the serpent that one day, a son would be born to a woman who would crush the serpent's head. God was already planning the comeback.

He knew that Adam and Eve could never fix the problem on their own. They couldn't "practice" hard enough to get back into the garden. They needed a Hero to come and win the game for them. This was the first time the Gospel, the Good News, was ever mentioned. Even in the middle of their biggest failure, God was showing them that he still loved them. He provided clothes for them and promised a way back, even though it would take a long time and a massive sacrifice.

Understanding the Opponent

To play a good game, you have to understand your opponent's tactics. The devil still uses the same tricks today that he used in the garden. He wants you to think that God's rules are meant to stop your fun. He wants you to believe that you can be your own king. He wants you to doubt that God really loves you.

When you feel those thoughts creeping in, remember Chapter 2. Remember that the serpent is a liar. God's boundaries are there to protect the "very good" life he designed for you. Sin always promises something great but leaves you hiding in the bushes, feeling ashamed. By learning how sin started, we can see why we need to stay close to our Coach. We can see that the only way to win is to trust the one who made the rules in the first place.

CHAPTER 3

SEE WHY PEOPLE NEED HELP

Think about a player who gets a serious injury during a game, like a torn ACL or a broken leg. No matter how much heart that player has, they cannot just "will" themselves to be healed. They cannot run a lap to fix a snapped bone. They need a surgeon. They need someone from the outside with the right tools to step in and repair what is broken. When sin entered the world, it wasn't just a small scratch or a minor penalty. It was a total system failure. The human race became "injured" in a way that we simply cannot fix by ourselves.

The Problem of a Broken Nature

Because of what happened in the garden, every person is now born with a natural pull toward doing things their own way instead of God's way. You might have noticed that nobody has to teach a toddler how to be selfish or how to scream "Mine!" when they want a toy. We don't have to take classes to learn how to lie or how to get jealous of a teammate who gets more playing time. Those things come naturally to us because our internal "compass" is broken.

The Bible uses a heavy word for this: dead. It says that without God's help, we are spiritually dead in our sins. A dead person cannot help themselves. A person at the bottom of a deep well without a ladder cannot just jump out, no matter how much they practice their vertical leap. This is why we need help. We aren't just good people who occasionally make mistakes; we are people with a deep heart problem that we cannot solve on our own.

The Trap of Being "Good Enough"

One of the biggest mistakes athletes make is thinking they can earn their way into God's favor by being better than the person next to them. We look at the "bad kids" or people who do terrible things and think, "Well, I'm doing okay. I follow the rules, I work hard, and I'm nice to my parents." We try to use our good deeds to balance out our bad ones, like trying to fix a failing grade by doing one extra credit assignment.

The problem is that God's standard isn't "better than average." His standard is 100 percent perfection. Imagine a basketball game where you have to make every single shot you take for your entire career, or you lose. One miss, and the game is over. That is what God's holiness requires. Even our very best days are still stained by selfish thoughts or pride. The Bible says our "righteous acts" are like filthy rags compared to God's purity. When we see how high the bar is, we realize that we are all stuck far below it.

Why We Can't Coach Ourselves Out

In sports, a good coach can help you fix your form or improve your speed. But a coach cannot change your heart. You can follow all the drills and learn all the plays, but if you still want to cheat when the ref isn't looking, the problem is still there. Religion often acts like a coach, giving us lists of "do's and don'ts." While those rules are good, they don't have the power to fix the "sin virus" inside us.

We need more than just a new set of rules; we need a new heart. We need a rescue that goes deeper than our actions. If we could have saved ourselves by being good, then Jesus wouldn't have had to die on the cross. The fact that the Son of God had to come and give his life is the ultimate proof that we were in a situation we couldn't handle. We were down by a million points with no time left on the clock, and we needed a miracle.

The Mirror of the Law

God gave us his laws, like the Ten Commandments, to act as a mirror. When you look in a mirror after a tough, muddy game, the mirror doesn't wash your face. It just shows you how dirty you are. The law shows us God's perfect standard so that we will stop trying to brag about ourselves and start looking for help. It reveals the gap between who we are and who God made us to be.

Acknowledging that you need help is actually the first step toward true strength. In a locker room, the player who hides an injury is a liability to the team. The player who admits they are hurt can get the treatment they need to get back in the game. Seeing why we need help isn't about feeling miserable; it's about being honest so that we can be healed.

The Need for a Substitute

Since we cannot hit the mark of perfection, we need someone else to do it for us. We need a "designated hitter" who can step up to the plate and knock it out of the park every single time. We need someone who can pay the penalty for our fouls so that we don't have to be kicked out of the game forever.

This is where the story starts to get exciting. Once you realize that you are completely stuck and unable to save yourself, you are finally ready to meet the Savior. You stop looking at your own "stats" and start looking at his. You stop trying to build your own ladder to heaven and start looking for the one God sent down to us. Help is available, but you have to admit that you need it before you can receive it.

Hope for the Injured

If you are feeling the weight of your own mistakes today, remember that God isn't surprised by your weakness. He knew you couldn't do it alone, and he never expected you to. He didn't give us a "do-it-yourself" kit for salvation. He gave us a Savior.

When you see why people need help, you stop judging others for their failures and start being thankful for God's grace. You realize that everyone is in the same boat. We are all "injured players" in need of a great Physician. This levels the playing field and makes us realize that we are all desperate for the same Hero. We were made for greatness, but we are currently broken, and that is exactly why Jesus came to find us.

CHAPTER 4

OWN YOUR NEED FOR A SAVIOR

In the world of sports, the hardest thing for a player to do is admit they can't handle a situation. We are coached from day one to be tough, to "grind it out," and to never show a hint of weakness to the opponent. But imagine a quarterback trying to play with a blind side he literally cannot see, or a pitcher whose arm is completely spent but refuses to call for the bullpen. If they keep pretending everything is fine, the whole team eventually pays the price.

The biggest "win" you will ever have in this life isn't a trophy or a scholarship. It is the moment you stop the act, drop the mask, and finally own the fact that you need a Savior. It's the moment you realize that "trying harder" is a dead end.

Stepping Out of the Huddle of Excuses

We all have a "huddle" of excuses we retreat to when we mess up. When we get caught in a lie, lose our temper on the court, or let pride get the best of us, our brain immediately starts running "defensive plays." We say things like, *I'm not as bad as that kid who got suspended,"* or *"I only acted that way because the ref was being unfair,"* or *"I'm just stressed out."* We try to explain away our sin because we desperately want to believe we are still the ones in control of our destiny. But owning your need for Jesus means stepping out of that huddle of excuses and standing alone before God. It means looking at the "foul" in your own heart—the hidden thoughts, the selfishness, the times you've ignored God—and saying, "I did this. This is on me." This isn't about beating yourself up or becoming a person who walks around with their head down. It's about being truthful. You can't be rescued from a situation you won't admit you are in. You have to sign your name to the "injury report" before the Great Physician can actually start the healing process.

The "I Can Do It Myself" Trap

The most dangerous person on any roster is the one who thinks they are bigger than the system. In our spiritual lives, we often try to be our own saviors. We tell ourselves that if we just practice more, go to church more often, or follow a list of "good person" rules, we can fix the "sin problem" through sheer willpower.

It's like trying to bail out a sinking boat with a plastic spoon. You're working incredibly hard, you're exhausted, and you might even look busy to the people watching from the shore, but you're still going down. Owning your need means dropping the spoon. It means admitting that your best effort on your best day will never be enough to reach the standard of a perfect and holy God. This is actually where true freedom starts. When you realize you can't save yourself, the crushing pressure to be perfect disappears. You stop trying to "earn" a spot on the roster and start realizing that Jesus has already bought your jersey, paid your league fees, and secured your place on the team.

A Personal Decision, Not a Team Move

You might have grown up in a house where the Bible is read every day. Your parents might be the strongest Christians you know, and your coaches might start every practice with a prayer. That is an incredible blessing, but you cannot live on their "stats." In sports, just because your dad was a Hall of Fame legend doesn't mean you automatically get a championship ring. You have to step onto the field yourself. You have to put in the work.

Owning your need for a Savior is a deeply personal decision. It is the moment where God stops being "the God of the Bible" or "the God my family talks about" and becomes **your** Savior. It's a one-on-one conversation between you and the King. It happens when the truth hits you: if you were the only person on earth, Jesus still would have walked to the cross just for you. You have to stop hiding in the crowd and step into the light.

The Unexpected Strength in Surrender

In our culture, the word "surrender" sounds like a total loss. It sounds like waving a white flag, hanging your head, and quitting the game. But in the Kingdom of God, surrender is the only way you actually win. When you surrender your life to Jesus, you aren't quitting; you are switching teams. You are moving from a team that is destined to lose, the team of "Self" and "Sin", to the team that has already won the final victory: the team of "Christ."

It takes way more courage to admit you need help than it does to keep faking it. It takes a real man or woman of God to stand up and say, "I am a sinner, I've messed up, and I cannot fix myself." When you own that need, God doesn't look at you with disappointment or give you a lecture. He looks at you with open arms. The Bible is clear: God opposes the proud, but he gives grace to the humble. If you want his power in your life, you have to start with humility. You have to admit you're out of your league.

Signing the Lifetime Contract

Think of this moment as signing your official contract with the King. When an athlete signs with a pro team, they are making a public statement: *"I am yours. I follow your playbook. I wear your colors. I trust your leadership over mine."* Owning your need for a Savior is you signing on the dotted line.

You are effectively telling God:

- **"I admit I've broken the rules."** You stop calling it "mistakes" and start calling it what God calls it: sin.

- **"I know I'm stuck."** You admit that no amount of "being a good kid" can bridge the gap between you and a holy God.

- **"I trust your work."** You believe that when Jesus died and rose again, he was doing it to pay the "fine" for your fouls.

- **"I'm handing over the ball."** You stop trying to be the MVP of your own life and you let Jesus be the Captain.

The Shift in Your Daily Game

Once you own your need, the way you play and live starts to change. You don't have to walk around with that heavy weight of shame anymore. Your "permanent record" is wiped totally clean because Jesus' perfect record has been credited to your account.

Now, when you make a mistake, and you will, you don't have to hide in the bushes like Adam and Eve did. You can go straight to your Savior, admit the foul, and get right back in the action. You are now playing with a new kind of confidence. You aren't playing *for* love or trying to *earn* God's approval; you are playing *from* a position of being totally loved. You know you are accepted, regardless of what the scoreboard says at the end of the day. This is the foundation for everything that comes next. You have faced the problem of sin, you have owned your need, and you are finally ready to walk with the Holy Spirit.

The Relief of Being Found

There is an old story about a sheep that gets lost and stuck in a thicket of thorns. The sheep can't get itself out; the more it struggles, the deeper the thorns go. It just has to wait for the shepherd to find it. Owning your need is like that sheep finally stopping its struggling and letting out a cry for help.

When the Shepherd finds you, he doesn't kick you for getting lost. He picks you up, puts you on his shoulders, and carries you back to the flock. That is what Jesus does when we own our need. He carries the weight that was crushing us. He brings us back to the place where we belong. You were made for greatness, and that greatness starts the moment you admit you can't reach it on your own.

SECTION FOUR

JOIN THE GREAT RESCUE

Every athlete knows the feeling of being recruited. There is a moment when a coach looks at you and says, "I want you on my team." They aren't just looking at your jersey; they are looking at your potential. Throughout the first three sections of this journey, we have looked at the "pre-game." We saw how God designed a perfect world, how sin threw a wrench into the gears, and how Jesus stepped onto the field as the ultimate Hero to win back what was lost.

But a victory on the field doesn't mean much if you aren't actually part of the team. This fourth part is about your invitation to join the greatest rescue mission in the history of the universe. This isn't just about knowing facts about God; it's about a relationship that changes how you wake up in the morning and how you compete in the afternoon. We are moving from the sidelines into the game.

Over the next four chapters, we are going to explore what it looks like to actually follow Jesus. We'll talk about "Grace", the gift you didn't earn. We'll talk about "Repentance", the decision to change your direction. We'll look at how to grow into the person God created you to be, and finally, how to take this message back to your teammates, your family, and your friends. The rescue is happening, and the Captain is calling your name.

CHAPTER 1

ACCEPT THE GIFT OF GRACE

Imagine you are trying out for the most elite team in the country. The standards are impossibly high. The coach is looking for a perfect 100% score on every drill. You show up, you give it everything you have, but at the end of the day, you know you didn't make the cut. You looked at the stats, and you're just not fast enough or strong enough. You're packing up your gear, feeling that heavy weight of failure, when the coach walks up to you. He hands you a team jersey with your name on it and says, "Welcome to the roster. Your spot is paid for."

You'd probably be confused. You'd say, "Coach, I didn't hit the numbers. I don't deserve this." And he would look you in the eye and say, "I know. But I'm giving it to you anyway."

That is **Grace**. In the world of sports, we are used to "merit." You get what you earn. You get playing time because you worked hard. You get a trophy because you won. But in the Kingdom of God, the most important thing you will ever receive is something you could never, ever earn.

The Definition of the Gift

Grace is a word we hear in church all the time, but we often miss how radical it really is. Grace is "unmerited favor." That's a fancy way of saying God gives us his best when we deserve his worst. To understand grace, you have to see it alongside two other words: Justice and Mercy.

- **Justice** is getting what you deserve. If you break a rule and get a penalty, that's justice.

- **Mercy** is *not* getting the punishment you deserve. If the ref sees the foul but lets you stay in the game, that's mercy.

- **Grace** is getting a reward you *didn't* earn. It's like committing a foul, being forgiven for it, and then being handed the MVP trophy anyway.

This goes against everything we are taught on the field. We are taught that "there's no such thing as a free lunch" and that "you get out what you put in." But if we got what we put in when it comes to God, we would all be disqualified. Grace is God's way of saying that the "score" between you and Him isn't based on your performance; it's based on Jesus' performance.

Why It Is Hard for Athletes to Accept

As an athlete, your whole life is built on performance. You are graded by your stats, your speed, and your wins. This makes accepting grace very difficult. Our pride wants to say, "I can do this myself." We want to feel like we earned our way to God. We want to be able to brag about how many chapters we read, how many times we prayed, or how "good" we are compared to the kids who get in trouble.

But the moment you try to "earn" God's love, you are stepping away from grace. Grace is a gift, and a gift can only be received, not bought. If you tried to pay your friend for a birthday present they gave you, it would be an insult. It would mean you don't want to be in their debt. We often do the same thing with God. We try to "pay him back" by being extra good. But grace says, "You can't pay me back. The price was already paid on the cross. Just take the gift."

The Power of the "Paid-in-Full" Contract

When a professional athlete signs a "guaranteed contract," it means their pay is locked in regardless of whether they have a bad game or get an injury. They can play with a sense of security because the deal is signed.

Accepting grace is like signing a guaranteed contract with God. Your "spot on the team" doesn't depend on how you feel on a Tuesday morning or whether you stumbled and sinned on a Friday night. It depends on the finished work of Jesus. When he said "It is finished" on the cross, he was signing the contract for you.

This doesn't mean we stop trying. In fact, it should make us work harder! A player with a guaranteed contract doesn't sit on the bench and eat chips; they play with a sense of freedom and joy because they aren't afraid of being cut. When you accept grace, you stop playing for *approval* and start playing *from* a place of being already approved.

The Mirror of Truth

To accept grace, you have to be honest about how much you need it. You have to look in the mirror and admit that you are "spiritually bankrupt." You have to realize that without Jesus, your score is zero.

This is the hardest part of the process. Our ego wants to believe we have at least a few "points" on the board. We want to think, "Sure, I'm a sinner, but I'm a *talented* sinner" or "I'm a *nice* sinner." But grace only flows to the humble. It's like a mountain: the water doesn't sit on the high, proud peaks; it flows down into the low valleys. If you want to experience the fullness of God's grace, you have to get low. You have to admit that you have nothing to offer him but your need.

Living Under the Waterfall

Imagine God's grace as a massive waterfall in the middle of a desert. You are thirsty, tired, and covered in dust from the "game" of life. You don't have to pay to get under the water. You don't have to prove you're a "good enough" runner to deserve the water. You just have to walk into it.

Accepting grace is a daily decision. It isn't just something that happens once when you're a kid. Every morning, you have to wake up and remind yourself: "I am a child of God not because of what I did yesterday, but because of what Jesus did 2,000 years ago." This keeps you humble when you win and hopeful when you lose. It protects you from the two biggest enemies of an athlete's soul: Pride (when you think you're the greatest) and Despair (when you think you're a failure).

Grace is Not a "Get Out of Jail Free" Card

Sometimes people hear about grace and think, "Cool, so I can just do whatever I want! If God's going to forgive me anyway, I might as well break the rules and have 'fun'."

But if you truly understand what grace cost, you would never think that way. Grace was "free" for you, but it cost Jesus everything. He had to pay the "fine" with his own life so you could get the gift. When you realize that the King of the universe died so you could be on his team, it makes you want to follow his rules more than ever. It creates a "heart of gratitude." You don't obey the Coach because you're afraid he'll kick you off the team; you obey him because you love him for letting you stay.

Right now, the Captain is calling you. He isn't asking for your stats. He isn't asking to see your highlight reel. He is looking at your heart and offering you the gift. He is offering you a clean slate, a new jersey, and a place in a Kingdom that will never end.

Will you stop trying to earn it? Will you drop the excuses and the pride? Accepting the gift of grace is the most "un-athletic" thing you will ever do, because it requires you to admit you can't win on your own. But it is the only way to join the Great Rescue. The jersey is held out toward you. All you have to do is take it.

CHAPTER 2

TURN AWAY FROM YOUR SIN

In the world of sports, there is a specific word that every player understands: **Adjustment**.

Imagine you are a pitcher, and every time you throw a fastball, the batter knocks it out of the park. Or imagine you are a soccer player, and you keep dribbling the ball into a crowd of defenders instead of passing to your open teammate. Your coach pulls you aside during a timeout and says, "You have to change what you're doing. If you keep going this way, you're going to lose the game."

At that moment, you have a choice. You can keep doing things your way, or you can "turn." You can adjust your stance, change your strategy, and head in a new direction. In the Bible, there is a special word for this kind of "about-face." It is called **Repentance**.

What Does Repentance Really Mean?

A lot of people think that repenting just means feeling bad or crying because you got caught doing something wrong. But if you get a penalty for tripping someone and you're only sorry because the referee saw you, that's not repentance—that's just being bummed out that you got a red card!

True repentance is like being on the wrong side of the field and realizing you're running toward the wrong goal. You don't just slow down; you stop, you turn around 180 degrees, and you start sprinting toward the right goal. It's a change of mind that leads to a change of action. It means saying to God, "I've been the captain of my own life, and I've been making a mess of it. I'm turning away from my way of doing things, and I'm turning toward Your way."

The "U-Turn" on the Field

Think of your life as a big field. Before you meet Jesus, you're usually playing for "Team Me." You want what you want, when you want it. You might be mean to a sibling because they annoyed you, or you might "fudge" the truth to your teacher to stay out of trouble. When we follow our own rules, we are heading away from God.

Repentance is the big U-turn. It's not just saying "I'm sorry" with your mouth; it's showing it with your feet. If you've been bullying a kid at school, repenting means you stop the bullying and start treating them with kindness. If you've been lazy and disrespectful to your parents, it means you turn toward being helpful and obedient. It's about changing teams. You leave "Team Me" and you join "Team Jesus."

The "Broken Play" of Sin

In football, a "broken play" is when everything goes wrong. The quarterback trips, the receivers run the wrong routes, and the ball ends up on the ground. Sin is like a broken play for your life. It messes up your relationship with God, it hurts the people around you, and it makes you feel heavy and sad inside.

God hates sin, but not because he's a "mean ref" who wants to ruin your fun. He hates sin because he loves you, and he knows that sin is like a poison that hurts his children. Turning away from sin is like dropping a heavy backpack that has been slowing you down during your sprints. God wants you to turn away from the bad stuff so you can be free to run the race he has planned for you.

Why Is It Hard to Turn?

Let's be honest: sometimes sin feels "fun" for a minute. It can feel good to win an argument by being mean, or to get something you want by being sneaky. That's why turning away is hard. It requires us to admit that our way of doing things is actually wrong.

In sports, it's hard to admit your technique is bad. You might have been shooting a basketball with the wrong form for years. When a coach tries to fix it, it feels weird and uncomfortable at first. You might even play worse for a day or two while you learn the new way. But if you want to be a champion, you have to trust the coach's correction. Turning away from sin feels "weird" at first because we are so used to our old, selfish habits. But as we practice following Jesus, the new way starts to feel like home.

The Secret Ingredient: God's Kindness

You might think that God is waiting for you to get perfect before he lets you turn to him. You might think he's standing there with a scowl, crossing his arms and waiting for you to "fix yourself." But the Bible tells us a secret: it is God's **kindness** that leads us to repentance.

Imagine a coach who sees you struggling. Instead of yelling and benching you, he puts his arm around your shoulder and says, "Hey, I know you're frustrated. Let me show you a better way to play. I'm not giving up on you." How would that make you feel? It would make you *want* to change! That is exactly how God treats us. He doesn't wait for us to be perfect. He loves us right where we are, and his love gives us the courage to turn around and head home.

You Don't Turn Alone

The coolest part about joining the Great Rescue is that you don't have to turn away from sin using only your own muscles. Remember the Holy Spirit we talked about? He is like your "Internal Coach." When you are tempted to do something wrong, he's the one who whispers to your heart, *"Hey, that's the wrong goal. Turn around!"* When you decide to repent, God gives you the power to actually do it. It's like having a turbo-boost on your U-turn. You provide the "Yes, I want to change," and God provides the strength to make the move. You aren't just trying harder; you are trusting more.

A Daily Adjustment

Repentance isn't just something you do once when you first become a Christian. It's something we do every single day. Just like a professional golfer makes tiny adjustments to their swing every time they hit the ball, we have to check our hearts every day.

Maybe you woke up in a bad mood and were grumpy at breakfast. That's a moment to stop, pray, and turn. *"Lord, I'm sorry for being grumpy. I want to be kind today. Help me turn back to You."* This keeps your heart "clean" and keeps you close to the Captain. It prevents the small mistakes from turning into big, game-ending fouls.

The Celebration in the Locker Room

Jesus told a story about a son who ran away and made a bunch of bad choices. When the son finally realized he was wrong, he turned around and headed back to his father. He thought his father would be angry, but instead, the father ran to him, hugged him, and threw a giant party!

Jesus says that every time one person turns away from sin and turns toward God, the angels in heaven have a massive celebration. It's like a locker room celebration after winning the Super Bowl. God isn't looking to punish you when you turn; he's looking to celebrate that his child is finally heading the right way.

Your Move

Are you running toward the wrong goal today? Is there something in your life, a lie, a bad attitude, or a secret habit, that you know isn't part of God's plan?

Don't be afraid to turn. Don't worry about being "perfect" first. Just stop, admit it to God, and make that U-turn. The Captain is standing there with his arms open, ready to help you run the right way. When you turn away from sin, you aren't losing anything valuable; you are gaining everything that matters. You're joining the rescue. You're getting back in the game.

CHAPTER 3

GROW IN YOUR NEW LIFE

Think about the day you first started playing your favorite sport. Maybe you were five years old, your jersey was three sizes too big, and you spent more time looking at the grass than at the ball. You were officially on the team, but you weren't a pro yet. You had the uniform, but you didn't have the skills. To get better, you had to go through a process. You had to show up to practice, listen to the coach, and do the same drills over and over again.

Following Jesus is exactly the same way. The moment you accept God's grace and decide to follow Him, you are "on the team." Your spot is safe. But that is just the beginning of the journey. God doesn't want you to stay a "rookie" forever. He wants you to grow, to get stronger, and to become a "veteran" in your faith. In the Bible, this process is called **Sanctification**. It's a big word, but it really just means "becoming more like Jesus every day."

The "Nutrition" of the Bible

If an athlete only eats candy and soda, they aren't going to have the energy to win a game. Their muscles will be weak, and they'll get tired in the first five minutes. To grow physically, you need good food. To grow spiritually, you need the "soul food" found in the Bible.

The Bible isn't just an old book of rules; it's God's playbook for your life. When you read it, you're letting the Coach speak directly to you. You start to learn how He thinks, what He loves, and how He wants you to handle tough situations.

Try to make it a habit to read a little bit of the Bible every day. You don't have to read ten chapters at a time. Even just a few verses can give you the "protein" you need to stay strong. When you read, ask yourself: *"What does this tell me about God?"* and *"How can I use this on the field today?"* The more you read, the more you'll start to think like a champion.

Staying in the Huddle: Prayer

Can you imagine a quarterback who never talks to the coach? Or a goalie who ignores the rest of the defenders? The team would be a mess! Communication is the key to any winning team. In your new life with Jesus, communication is called **Prayer**.

Prayer isn't a magic spell, and it doesn't have to be fancy. It's just talking to God like He's your best friend or your favorite coach. You can pray anywhere—in the locker room before a big game, on the bus, or while you're laying in bed at night.

- **Thank Him:** "Lord, thanks for giving me the strength to play today."

- **Ask for Help:** "Coach, I'm feeling really nervous about this game. Help me to be brave."

- **Own Your Fouls:** "I'm sorry I lost my temper at practice. Help me to be a better teammate tomorrow."

When you stay in constant communication with God, you'll start to feel His peace and His guidance. You'll realize that you're never playing the game alone.

The Power of Practice: Discipline

Nobody becomes a superstar overnight. It takes thousands of hours of practice. You have to do the "boring" stuff, like running laps or practicing your footwork, so that when the big moment comes, you're ready. Growing in your faith takes discipline, too.

Discipline means doing the right thing even when you don't feel like it. There will be days when you don't feel like being kind. There will be days when you'd rather sleep in than pray. But just like a dedicated athlete gets out of bed for a 6:00 AM practice, a follower of Jesus makes time for the things that help them grow.

Every time you choose to tell the truth when it's hard, or every time you choose to encourage a teammate instead of complaining, you are "leveling up." You are building spiritual muscles that will help you stay strong when life gets difficult.

Don't Play Solo: The Team (Church)

You can practice by yourself in your driveway for hours, but you can't play a real game alone. You need a team. In your walk with God, that team is the **Church**.

The church isn't just a building; it's a group of people who are all heading toward the same goal. When you're part of a church or a youth group, you have teammates who can cheer you up when you're down and challenge you to be better. We need each other! Sometimes you'll be the one helping a friend understand a Bible verse, and sometimes a friend will be the one helping you through a tough week. When we stand together, we are much harder to beat.

Handling the "Losing Streaks"

Even the best teams in the world lose sometimes. Even the best Christians mess up. You might have a week where you're grumpy, you ignore your Bible, and you say something mean. When that happens, the enemy (the devil) will whisper to you: *"See? You're not a real Christian. You haven't grown at all. You might as well just quit."*

Don't listen to that! Growth isn't a perfectly straight line up. It's more like a series of ups and downs that slowly heads higher. When you fall, don't stay down. Admit your mistake to God, accept His grace (remember Chapter 1?), and get back to practice. A "loss" is only a total failure if you refuse to learn from it and keep going.

Watching for the "Fruit"

How do you know if you're actually growing? In an apple tree, you look for apples. In a follower of Jesus, you look for what the Bible calls the **Fruit of the Spirit**.

As you grow, you'll notice that you are becoming more loving, joyful, peaceful, patient, kind, good, faithful, gentle, and self-controlled. You'll realize that you don't get as angry as you used to when things don't go your way. You'll find yourself wanting to help others more than you want to help yourself. That is the Holy Spirit working in you! It's like seeing your "stats" improve over the course of a season. It's proof that the Coach is doing a great work in your heart.

Growth takes time. You won't be a spiritual giant by next Tuesday. It's a "long game" that lasts your whole life. The goal isn't to be perfect; the goal is to be closer to Jesus today than you were yesterday.

So, keep showing up. Keep "eating" the Word. Keep talking to the Coach. Keep leaning on your teammates. You are part of the Great Rescue, and God is committed to helping you grow into the incredible person He designed you to be. You're not just an athlete anymore; you're a child of the King, and your future is brighter than any championship trophy!

CHAPTER 4

SPREAD THE MESSAGE OF HOPE

Imagine you've spent your whole life practicing on a court with broken rims and flat balls. Then, one day, a scout shows up and brings you to a state-of-the-art stadium. The grass is perfect, the equipment is brand new, and the Coach is the greatest to ever live. Not only that, but he tells you that your spot is guaranteed and the snacks are free. What is the very first thing you're going to do? You aren't going to sit in the dugout and keep it to yourself. You're going to run back to your old neighborhood, find all your friends who are still struggling with those flat basketballs, and say, "You won't believe what I found! There's a place for you here, too!"

That is the heart of spreading the message of hope. In the Bible, this is often called **The Great Commission**. It sounds like a heavy, formal term, but in sports language, it's simply the "Post-Game Interview" that lasts for the rest of your life. It's the moment the Coach gives you the playbook and says, "The rescue is for everyone. Now, go and get the rest of the team."

The Strategy: Living as a Human Billboard

In the world of professional sports, companies pay millions of dollars to put their logos on jerseys. Why? Because they know that if you admire an athlete, you'll look at what they're wearing. You are a "brand ambassador" for the Kingdom of God. Before you ever open your mouth to talk about a Bible verse, people are reading the "logo" of your life.

Think about the high-pressure moments of a game. When the referee makes a call that is clearly wrong—a call that might cost you the game—how do you react? If you blow up, scream, and throw your helmet, you're sending a message. But if you show self-control, even when it hurts, you're sending a different message. People start to wonder, *"What does he have that I don't? Why isn't he falling apart right now?"*

Being a "Human Billboard" means your character becomes the advertisement for God's grace. It means being the hardest worker on the field, not because you're trying to show off, but because you're playing for a higher King. It means being the person who stays late to help the manager pick up the cones, or the one who sits with the new kid on the bench who doesn't have any friends yet. These small, daily actions create "curiosity." They earn you the right to be heard when you finally do speak.

Developing Your "Scouting Report" (Your Testimony)

Every great player has a scouting report—a summary of where they came from, what their strengths are, and how they play the game. In your spiritual life, your scouting report is your **Testimony**. This is simply the story of your journey with Jesus.

A lot of kids think, *"My story is boring. I wasn't a bank robber who became a preacher. I'm just a middle-schooler who likes baseball."* But here is a secret: your story is exactly what someone else needs to hear. Most people aren't looking for a movie-star miracle; they are looking for a reason to have peace when they fail a math test or lose a championship game.

To build your testimony, think of it in three "quarters":

1. **First Quarter: The Need.** What was your life like before you really understood God's love? Maybe you felt like you had to be perfect to be loved. Maybe you were really lonely or had a quick temper.

2. **Second Quarter: The Turn.** How did you realize you needed a Savior? Was it a talk with a coach, a verse you read, or just a feeling in your heart that there had to be more to life?

3. **Third Quarter: The New Life.** How is your life different now? You still have problems, and you still lose games, but what has changed on the *inside*? Do you have more joy? Is it easier to forgive people?

When you share your story, you aren't giving a lecture. You're just sharing your "highlight reel." You are saying, "I was lost on the field, I found the Coach, and now I'm part of the rescue."

The "Invite" Play: Breaking the Ice

Sometimes, we think spreading the message means standing on a table in the cafeteria and shouting. While that's brave, it's usually not the most effective way to reach your teammates. Most "recruiting" happens in the quiet moments—on the back of the bus, in the weight room, or while you're stretching before practice.

The "Invite" Play is simple. It's about looking for "openings" in a conversation.

- **The "Me Too" Opening:** If a teammate says, "I'm so stressed about this season," you can say, "Man, I totally get that. I used to feel the same way until I started realize that my value isn't just in my stats. My church group talks about this stuff—you should come with me sometime."

- **The "Prayer" Opening:** If someone is going through a hard time, like a divorce in their family or an injury, you can simply say, "I'm really sorry you're going through that. I'm going to be praying for you." Most people—even if they don't believe in God yet—will be touched that you care enough to pray.

- **The "Question" Opening:** Sometimes, just asking a question is the best way. "Do you ever think about God or what happens after we die?" This isn't being pushy; it's being curious.

Handling the "Benchings" and Rejections

In sports, you're going to get rejected. You're going to try out for a team and get cut. You're going to take a shot and miss. The same thing happens when you share the message of hope. Some people will think it's "weird." Some people might make a joke at your expense.

When this happens, you have to remember the "Final Score." You aren't responsible for how people respond; you are only responsible for being a faithful messenger. If someone says "no" to an invite, it doesn't mean you failed. It just means the "timing" wasn't right. God is the one who does the heavy lifting of changing people's hearts. Your job is just to keep the door open. Stay kind. Don't get defensive. If you stay a great teammate even after they say "no," you're proving that your love for them isn't "fake." It shows them that you care about *them*, not just about "winning an argument."

Teamwork: Building a Huddle

You shouldn't try to be a lone scout. The Great Commission is a team effort. If there are other Christians on your team or in your school, find them! There is incredible power in a "Huddle."

Think about starting a small group before practice once a week. It doesn't have to be long—just ten minutes. Read one verse, talk about how it applies to your sport, and pray for your team. When other players see a group of athletes who are united, disciplined, and full of joy, they will naturally want to know what's going on. A "Huddle" provides a safe place for people to ask questions and see that following Jesus isn't just for "quiet people"—it's for competitors, too.

The Global Rescue: Looking Beyond the Field

While your primary "mission field" is your current team, the message of hope is meant for the whole world. Part of spreading the message is caring about what God is doing in other places.

Maybe your team can do a service project together, like cleaning up a local park or volunteering at a food bank. Maybe you can save up some of your own money to help support a missionary who is bringing the message of hope to a country where people have never heard of Jesus. When you look beyond your own "stats" and start caring about the "global score," your heart gets bigger. You realize that you are part of a massive, worldwide movement of rescue.

Dealing with the "I'm Not Good Enough" Fear

The biggest reason kids don't share their faith is that they feel like "hypocrites." They think, *I can't tell people about Jesus because I just got a yellow card for yelling at the ref last week,"* or *"I'm not a perfect student, so they won't listen to me."*

Here is the truth: **The world doesn't need to see a perfect Christian; they need to see a forgiven one.** If you pretend to be perfect, people will find you annoying and fake. But if you are honest about your mistakes, if you go to a teammate and say, "Hey, I'm sorry I was a jerk at practice yesterday; I'm still learning how to let God control my temper", that is incredibly powerful. It shows people that Christianity isn't a "club for perfect people." It's a "hospital for the broken." Your honesty about your struggles is actually one of your best tools for spreading hope.

The Power of Words (and the Silence)

The Bible says that the tongue has the power of life and death. As an athlete, your words carry weight. You can use your words to "trash talk" and tear people down, or you can use them to "speak life."

Spreading the message of hope means being the person who speaks up for the kid who is being bullied. It means being the one who shuts down gossip in the locker room. It means using your social media to post things that encourage others rather than just showing off your own highlights. Every time you use your words for good, you are pushing back the darkness and letting the light of the Kingdom shine through.

The Finish Line: Why We Do It

Why do we go through the trouble of sharing this message? Because we know the "Final Score" of history. We know that Jesus is coming back to fix everything. We know that there is a real Heaven and a real Hell, and we want as many people as possible to be on the winning team.

When you stand at the end of your life, you won't be thinking about how many points you scored in eighth grade. You'll be thinking about the people you helped. You'll be thinking about the teammate who started going to church because of you, or the friend who found hope in their darkest hour because you shared your story.

A Call to Action: Your Next Play

So, what is your next play?

1. **Identify your "Target":** Who is one person on your team or in your life who needs hope right now?

2. **Pray for the Opening:** Ask God to give you a chance to say something encouraging or to share a piece of your story.

3. **Be Ready:** Keep your "jersey" clean. Live in a way that makes people curious about your Captain.

4. **Speak Up:** When the moment comes, don't be afraid. The Holy Spirit will give you the words to say.

You are part of the Great Rescue. You aren't just an athlete; you are a messenger of the King. The world is full of people who are playing on flat courts with broken hearts. You know where the Great Stadium is. You know the Coach. Now, go and bring them home.

CONCLUSION

LIVE FOR THE GLORY OF GOD

You have reached the end of the manual, but in the Kingdom of God, the finish line of one season is always the starting blocks for the next. We have journeyed through the architecture of the universe, the tragedy of the fall, the rescue of the Cross, and the power of the Spirit. Now, we face the most important question any competitor can ask: **"Now what?"**

How do you take these truths into a locker room that smells like sweat and echoes with trash talk? How do you hold onto your faith when you're exhausted, your muscles are screaming, and you just lost the biggest game of your life? The answer is found in a single, life-altering phrase: **Living for the glory of God.**

Pillar 1: The Definition of the Goal

In sports, "glory" is usually something we try to steal for ourselves. We want the highlight reel to be about us. We want the "likes" on social media. We want the scholarship. But the Bible tells us that glory belongs to God alone. The word "glory" in the original Hebrew is *kavod*, which literally means "heaviness" or "weight."

When you live for God's glory, you are telling the world that God is the "Heaviest" thing in your life. He carries more weight than your coach's opinion, more weight than the scouts' reports, and even more weight than your own feelings of success or failure.

The Mirror Principle

Imagine a mirror. A mirror is a wonderful tool, but it has no light of its own. If you put a mirror in a pitch-black room, it shows nothing. But if you hold that mirror up to the sun, it becomes blindingly bright. It reflects the sun's glory into the dark corners of the world.

You are that mirror. You aren't the Sun. You aren't the source of the talent, the breath in your lungs, or the beating of your heart. Your job as a Christian athlete is to "reflect" the greatness of the Creator. When people see your hard work, your integrity, and your kindness, they shouldn't just think, *"Wow, he's a great player."* They should think, *"Wow, his God must be incredible."*

Pillar 2: The Psychology of a God-Centered Competitor

Most athletes are driven by a "Performance Identity." This means their happiness is tied to their stats. If they score, they feel like a king. If they miss, they feel like a failure. This is a roller coaster that eventually breaks everyone.

Playing from Victory, Not for Victory

Living for God's glory changes your "Why." You no longer play to *get* an identity; you play *from* an identity.

- **The Old Way:** "I need to win so that I am worthy of love."
- **The New Way:** "I am already perfectly loved by the King of the Universe; therefore, I can play with total freedom."

This freedom is your greatest competitive advantage. An athlete who isn't afraid to lose is the most dangerous person on the field. Why? Because they aren't "tight." They aren't choked by anxiety. They can take the big shot or make the risky play because they know their "Final Score" is already settled in Heaven.

Pillar 3: The Ethics of the Field

How does a "Glory-First" athlete handle the "Dirty" side of sports? We live in a world that says, *"It's only a foul if the ref sees it,"* or *"If you aren't cheating, you aren't trying."*

Integrity in the Dark

Living for God's glory means recognizing that there are no "secret" plays. God sees the way you talk to the bench players when the coach isn't listening. He sees the way you handle yourself in the bottom of a pile-up.

A "Glory-First" athlete values **Integrity** over **Image**.

- **Image** is who people *think* you are based on your stats and your social media.
- **Integrity** is who you *actually* are when the cameras are off and the stands are empty.

When you refuse to cheat, even when it would guarantee a win, you are saying that God's approval matters more than a trophy. That is how you make God look "Heavy" and "Important."

Pillar 4: The Theology of Training

Many people think that "God stuff" only happens when you're praying or in church. But God is the one who created your muscles, your tendons, and your nervous system. He is the one who designed the laws of physics that allow a ball to curve or a runner to accelerate.

Training as Worship

Every rep in the weight room can be a prayer. Every mile you run can be an act of gratitude. When you push your body to its limits, you are honoring the "Equipment" God gave you.

- **Laziness** is a form of ingratitude. It's like being given a Ferrari and letting it rust in the rain.
- **Excellence** is a form of worship. It's saying, *"God, You gave me this body and this opportunity, and I'm going to use it to the max to show how great Your creation is."*

This doesn't mean you have to be the best in the world. It means you have to be the best *you* that God created you to be.

Pillar 5: Dealing with Injuries and Setbacks

One of the hardest parts of being an athlete is when the "game" is taken away from you. An injury can feel like a death. It can feel like God has forgotten you.

The Glory in the Waiting Room

If you can only glorify God when you're winning, your god is actually your own success. But if you can glorify God while sitting on the sidelines with an ice pack on your knee, you have found the real secret.

In the "Waiting Room" of an injury, God is often doing a deeper work. He is teaching you that you are more than just an athlete. He is teaching you to find your joy in Him, not in your jersey. When your teammates see you staying positive and encouraging them even when you can't play, you are providing a testimony that is more powerful than a thousand touchdowns. You are showing them that your hope is "unshakeable."

Pillar 6: The Community of the Kingdom

Sports can be a very lonely world. It's all about "me" and "my" career. But as we saw in section 4, we are called to a "Huddle."

Being a "Great Commission" Teammate

You aren't on your team by accident. God didn't just "luck" you into that roster. You are a missionary in a jersey.

- **The Servant Leader:** Jesus said that the greatest in the kingdom is the servant of all. Be the player who picks up the equipment. Be the one who stays late to help a struggling teammate.

- **The Truth-Speaker:** Have the courage to speak up when something wrong is happening. If there's bullying or "locker room talk" that degrades people, be the one who says, *"We're better than that."*

Pillar 7: The Final Whistle

Every career ends. Whether it ends in high school, college, or the pros, the day will come when you hang up your cleats for the last time.

Playing for the Eternal Trophy

If you live for the glory of God, you never have to fear the "End." You aren't playing for a trophy that will gather dust or a record that will be broken. You are playing for a Crown of Life that lasts forever.

When you get to the end of your life, the goal is to look back and see a trail of people who were helped, a legacy of integrity, and a heart that stayed close to the Coach. You want to hear those words: *"Well done, good and faithful servant."*

Final Call to Action

The world is full of "Regular" athletes. The world is full of people who play for themselves. But the world is starving for "Resurrection Athletes."

- Be the player who loves the unlovable.
- Be the player who is honest when it costs them.
- Be the player who works harder than everyone else because they're playing for a King.

The "Great Rescue" is happening right now. It's happening in your school, in your gym, and on your field. You have the playbook. You have the Holy Spirit. You have the Captain on your side.

Now, get out there and live for the glory of God.

THE JUNIOR THEOLOGIAN'S ACTION MANUAL

Putting the "Big Truths" to Work

Systematic Theology is like a blueprint. A blueprint is a beautiful drawing of a house, but you can't live inside a piece of paper. You have to take the instructions on that paper and start laying bricks, installing windows, and turning on the lights.

This section shows you how to "live inside" the truth. We are going to look at five major "rooms" of theology and see how to put them into action right now.

Room 1: The Doctrine of God (Theology Proper)

Topic: The Omniscience and Omnipresence of God

The Big Idea: God knows everything (Omniscience) and is everywhere at the same time (Omnipresence).

1. The "Secret Truth" Action

Have you ever felt like nobody really "gets" you? Maybe you're sad, but you don't have the words to explain why. Or maybe you did something really kind, but nobody saw it.

- **In Action:** Because God is Omniscient, He is the only person who knows exactly how you feel. You never have to explain yourself to Him. When you're lonely, you can say, "God, You know exactly how I feel, and You are right here with me."
- **The Practice:** Spend five minutes tonight talking to God about your "secrets"—not just the bad things, but the dreams and the quiet thoughts you have. Knowing He is already there makes prayer feel less like a speech and more like a conversation with a friend who already knows the ending of your sentences.

2. The "Fear-Fighter" Action

When the lights are off and the house is quiet, it's easy to feel small and afraid. But Theology Proper tells us God has no "edges."

- **In Action:** Omnipresence means God isn't "watching from a distance." He is closer to you than your own shadow.
- **The Practice:** Memorize **Psalm 139:7-10**. Next time you feel nervous, whether it's a dark room or a big test, remind yourself: "There is nowhere I can go where God is not."

Room 2: The Doctrine of Man (Anthropology)

Topic: The Imago Dei (The Image of God)

The Big Idea: Every human being is a "mirror" designed to reflect God's glory.

1. The "Dignity" Action

In middle school, it's easy to judge people by what they wear, how smart they are, or how good they are at sports. But Anthropology tells us that every person is a "Masterpiece" because they carry God's image.

- **In Action:** This changes how you treat the kid who sits alone at lunch or the neighbor who seems "weird." You don't be nice to them because you're a "good person"; you be nice to them because you are respecting the Artist who made them.

- **The Practice:** The "Masterpiece Mission." This week, find one person who is usually ignored. Look them in the eye and say "Hello" or ask them a question. Remind yourself: *"This person is a living, breathing reflection of the King."*

2. The "Self-Worth" Action

Sometimes we look in the mirror and don't like what we see. We wish we were taller, thinner, or faster.

- **In Action:** If you are an Image-Bearer, your value doesn't come from your "stats." It comes from your "Designer."

- **The Practice:** Write down three things you *can* do (like drawing, listening, or being funny). Next to them, write how those things reflect God (He is the Ultimate Creator, the Ultimate Listener, the Creator of Joy).

Room 3: The Doctrine of Christ (Christology)

Topic: The Prophet, Priest, and King

The Big Idea: Jesus is our perfect Teacher (Prophet), our Helper (Priest), and our Leader (King).

1. The "Advice" Action (Jesus as Prophet)

When you have a big decision to make, like whether to tell the truth when it's hard, you need a Prophet to tell you God's words.

- **In Action:** Instead of just asking your friends what they think, go to the "Head Prophet."

- **The Practice:** Open your Bible to the "Red Letters" (the words of Jesus). Find one thing Jesus said about being honest or kind. That is your "Direct Order" for the day.

2. The "Brave" Action (Jesus as King)

Sometimes we feel like the "bad guys" (sin, bullies, or scary thoughts) are winning.

- **In Action:** Because Jesus is King, He is in charge of the whole universe. He has already defeated the biggest enemies (Sin and Death).

- **The Practice:** When you feel overwhelmed, picture a King on a throne who is also your best friend. Tell Him, "King Jesus, please handle this problem for me. I'm on Your team."

Topic: Justification and Adoption

The Big Idea: God declares us "Not Guilty" (Justification) and makes us His children (Adoption).

1. The "Fresh Start" Action

When you mess up, like losing your temper or lying, you might feel like a "failure." You might want to hide from God.

- **In Action:** Justification means God has already looked at your "record" and written **PAID** in big red letters because of Jesus.
- **The Practice:** The "Eraser Prayer." When you sin, don't wait three days to pray. Go to God immediately. Confess it, and then *believe* that it is gone. Don't keep carrying the guilt around. A justified person walks with their head up!

2. The "Family" Action

A lot of kids feel like they have to "earn" their parents' or teachers' love by being good.

- **In Action:** Adoption means God is your Father forever. You didn't "earn" your way into His family, so you can't "lose" your way out of it by having a bad day.
- **The Practice:** Every morning this week, say out loud: "I am a child of the King, and He is proud of me today." See how that changes your confidence!

Room 5: The Doctrine of the Church (Ecclesiology)

Topic: The Body of Christ

The Big Idea: We are all different parts of one "Body," and we need each other.

1. The "No-Jealousy" Action

When you see a friend get a new bike or get an "A" on a test, it's easy to feel jealous.

- **In Action:** If the "Hand" wins a trophy, the "Foot" should celebrate too, because they are on the same body!
- **The Practice:** The "Teammate Cheer." This week, when something good happens to someone else, be the first person to tell them "Great job!" without wishing it had happened to you.

2. The "Helping Hand" Action

You might think you're "too young" to help the church.

- **In Action:** Every part of the body has a job. If the pinky finger stopped working, the hand would be weaker.

- **The Practice:** Ask your parents or your church leader: "Is there one small thing I can do to help this week?" It could be picking up trash, holding a door, or writing a "Get Well" card to someone who is sick.

Room 6: The Junior Theologian's "Daily Briefing"

To stay sharp, a Theologian needs a daily routine. Here is a 5-minute plan to keep your "System" running smoothly:

1. **The Look Up (1 Minute):** Remind yourself of one Attribute of God. ("God, You are Immutable. You never change.")

2. **The Look In (1 Minute):** Be honest about your "Humanity." ("I am a sinner, and I need Your grace today.")

3. **The Look at Christ (1 Minute):** Thank Jesus for His "Offices." ("Thank You for being my Priest and praying for me.")

4. **The Look Out (2 Minutes):** Treat someone like an "Image-Bearer." (Think of one person you will be kind to today.)

Summary for the Junior Theologian

Theology isn't a dusty book on a high shelf. It is the "software" that runs your life. When you understand **who God is**, **who you are**, and **what Jesus did**, the world stops being a confusing place. You start to see the "Logic of Love" everywhere.

You are no longer just a kid living day-to-day. You are a **Theologian in Training**, helping God build His kingdom right where you are: in your school, in your living room, and in your heart.

THE JUNIOR THEOLOGIAN'S GUIDE TO BIG EMOTIONS

How Your Feelings Fit Into God's Big Plan

Have you ever felt like your emotions are a wild roller coaster? One minute you're at the top, laughing and feeling like you can conquer the world (Joy). The next minute, you're plunging down into a dark tunnel because someone said something mean (Sadness), or your heart is racing because you're worried about a big presentation at school (Fear).

As a Junior Theologian, you might wonder: *"Does God care about my feelings? Are some emotions 'sinful'? Why did God even give us feelings if they hurt so much sometimes?"*

Theology teaches us that God is the **Author of Emotions**. He isn't a robot, and He didn't design you to be one either. Because you are made in the **Image of God**, your ability to feel deeply is actually a gift.

However, because of the **Fall**, our "Feeling-Thermometer" is sometimes broken. This section will help you understand how to handle your "Big Feelings" using the blueprint of Systematic Theology.

1. The Theology of Joy (Reflecting God's Happiness)

The Big Idea: God is the happiest Being in the universe, and He made you to find your ultimate joy in Him.

In Systematic Theology, we learn about God's **Beatitude**. That's a fancy word that means God is perfectly happy and satisfied within Himself. When you feel a burst of joy because you're playing with a puppy, eating your favorite ice cream, or finishing a hard project, you are reflecting a tiny bit of God's own happiness.

- **The Problem:** Because of sin, we often try to find joy in things that don't last. We think, "If I just get that new video game, I'll be happy forever." But that joy eventually fades.
- **The Action Manual:** Junior Theologians practice **Gratitude**. Instead of just enjoying the "gift," we look up at the "Giver."
- **The Practice:** The "Joy-Trace." When you feel happy today, stop and "trace" that feeling back to God. Say, "God, thank You for this fun moment. Thank You that You are the source of all good things!"

2. The Theology of Sadness (God's Heart for a Broken World)

The Big Idea: Sadness is not a "bad" emotion; it is a sign that we know the world is not the way God originally designed it to be.

Did you know that Jesus cried? In the Gospel of John, when His friend Lazarus died, the Bible says, "Jesus wept." This is a huge theological truth! It means that God is not "above" our sadness. He is a **High Priest** who can sympathize with our weaknesses.

- **The Problem:** Sometimes sadness can make us want to hide from God or think that He is being mean.
- **The Action Manual:** Junior Theologians use **Lament**. Lament is a "prayer in the rain." It is talking to God about your sadness instead of just sitting in it.

- **The Practice:** The "Honest Prayer." If you are sad, tell God exactly why. *"God, my heart hurts because my friend moved away. I know You are a Comforter. Please hold me close today."*

3. The Theology of Anger (The Defense of What is Right)

The Big Idea: Anger was designed to be our "Alarm System" against things that are wrong and unjust.

In Theology Proper, we learn about **God's Holy Wrath**. God gets angry at sin, bullying, and lies because those things hurt the people He loves. Anger, in its purest form, is meant to make us want to fix what is broken.

- **The Problem:** Because of our "Total Depravity," our anger usually turns into **Sinful Anger**. We get mad because we didn't get our way, or we want to hurt someone back. This is called "Selfish Anger."

- **The Action Manual:** Junior Theologians practice **Self-Control** (a Fruit of the Spirit). Before you react in anger, ask yourself: *"Am I mad because God's rules were broken, or just because I'm not getting my way?"*

- **The Practice:** The "Cool-Down Countdown." When you feel the "heat" of anger, stop and count to ten while saying, *"God is the Judge, not me."* This gives your heart a second to switch from "Selfish Anger" to "Seeking Justice."

4. The Theology of Fear (Trusting the Sovereignty of God)

The Big Idea: Fear is a reminder that we are small and that we need a Protector who is much bigger than we are.

Systematic Theology teaches us about God's **Sovereignty**. This means God is in total control of every atom and every second of time. Fear happens when we forget who is on the throne. We feel like the world is "out of control," and we are afraid of what might happen.

- **The Problem:** Fear can paralyze us. It can make us stop doing the good things God has called us to do.

- **The Action Manual:** Junior Theologians practice **Trust**. We don't try to "stop feeling afraid"; we just "start trusting the King."

- **The Practice:** The "Scripture Shield." Choose one verse about God's power (like **Joshua 1:9**). When fear knocks on your door, answer it with that verse. Say, *"I am afraid, but my God is Sovereign, and He is with me."*

5. The Theology of Peace (The Result of Justification)

The Big Idea: Peace is not just the "absence of trouble"; it is the "presence of God."

Because of **Justification**, we have "Peace with God." The war between us and God is over! This theological truth should create a deep, quiet sense of "okay-ness" in our hearts, even when the world outside is noisy.

- **The Problem:** We often think peace comes from having a perfect life with no homework and no chores. That is "False Peace."

- **The Action Manual:** Junior Theologians practice **Stillness**.

- **The Practice:** The "Bedtime Hand-Off." Every night, imagine you are holding all your big feelings in your hands like a heavy bag. In your mind, "hand" that bag to Jesus. Say, *"Lord, You are in charge of tomorrow. I'm going to rest in Your peace."*

Putting it All Together: The Heart-Check

To keep your emotions in line with your theology, try the **Junior Theologian Heart-Check** once a day. Ask yourself these three questions:

1. **What am I feeling?** (Identify the emotion: Joy, Sad, Mad, or Scared).

2. **What is the truth?** (Remind yourself of a Doctrine: God is in control, God is Love, or God is the Judge).

3. **What is my move?** (Decide to Praise, Lament, Forgive, or Trust).

When you do this, your feelings stop being your "boss" and start being your "servant." They help you see God more clearly. You aren't just a kid with "moods"; you are a child of God learning to feel the way your Father feels.

EXTRA CONTENT
THE GREAT SYSTEMATIC THEOLOGY MEGA-QUIZ

Level: Junior Theologian Certification

Congratulations! You have traveled through the most important truths in the universe. You've looked at the blueprint of creation, the rescue mission of Jesus, and the action plan for your feelings. But how much of that "System" stayed in your brain?

It's time to put your knowledge to the test. This isn't a boring school test; it's a **Scouting Report** for your soul. Grab a piece of paper, find a quiet spot, and let's see if you're ready for your Junior Theologian Certification! (*Read until the end to get your answers!*)

In this level, we test what you know about God's Nature and our Design.

1. The "I AM" Mystery When God told Moses His name was "I AM WHO I AM," what was He teaching us about Himself?

- A) That He is forgetful and couldn't remember His name.
- B) That He is "Self-Existent" (Aseity) and doesn't need anything else to live.
- C) That He only likes short names.
- D) That He is a mystery that no one can ever talk to.

2. True or False: The Changing God God sometimes changes His mind about His promises if we have a really bad day.

3. The Attribute Match-Up Match the "Big Word" on the left with its kid-friendly definition on the right:

1. Omniscience	A. God is everywhere at the same time.
2. Omnipotence	B. God never, ever changes.
3. Omnipresence	C. God knows every fact and every thought.
4. Immutability	D. God has all the power in the universe.

4. The "Imago Dei" Detective If you see a classmate being teased because they are different from everyone else, which doctrine should pop into your head to tell you that bullying is wrong?

A) The Doctrine of Sleep.

B) The Doctrine of the Image of God (Imago Dei).

C) The Doctrine of Clouds.

D) The Doctrine of Math.

5. The Ink in the Water In Chapter 2, we talked about "Total Depravity." What does that mean for us?

A) We are as mean and bad as we could possibly be.

B) We are 100% perfect.

C) Sin has touched every part of us (mind, heart, and body), like ink in a glass of water.

D) We only sin when we are hungry.

In this level, we see if you understand the "Person and Work" of Jesus.

6. The 100/100 Rule Theology teaches us about the "Hypostatic Union." This means Jesus is:

    A) 50% God and 50% Man.

    B) 100% God and 100% Man at the same time.

    C) A man who worked really hard until God made Him a god.

    D) An angel wearing a human costume.

7. The Three Offices Jesus has three "jobs" or "offices." Which one describes Jesus as the one who speaks God's words to us perfectly?

    A) The King.

    B) The Priest.

    C) The Prophet.

    D) The Principal.

8. Scenario Challenge: The Scared Heart Imagine you are very afraid of something that might happen next week. If you remember that Jesus is your **King**, how does that help you?

    A) It reminds me that I should buy a crown.

    B) It reminds me that Jesus is in control of the whole universe and is stronger than my fear.

    C) It reminds me that I should try to be my own king.

    D) It doesn't help at all.

9. The Priest's Job In the Old Testament, a Priest offered sacrifices for the people. How did Jesus fulfill the "Office of Priest"?

    A) He built a giant temple out of gold.

    B) He offered Himself as the perfect sacrifice to pay for our sins.

    C) He told everyone to be nicer to each other.

    D) He became a judge in a courtroom.

In this level, we check your knowledge of how we are saved and how the Church works.

10. The Great Exchange In the "Action Manual," we learned about Justification. What is the "Great Exchange"?

    A) Trading your old bike for a new one.

    B) Jesus taking our sin and giving us His perfect righteousness.

    C) Trading lunch snacks at school.

    D) God taking our good deeds and giving us a trophy.

11. Adoption Papers Because of salvation, God becomes our "Father." This is called "Adoption." What is one benefit of being adopted into God's family?

    A) You never have to do chores again.

    B) You are a child of the King, and you can't "lose" your place in the family.

    C) You get to move to a castle tomorrow.

    D) You are better than everyone else who isn't adopted.

12. The Body of Christ Puzzle If the "Eye" in the church is jealous of the "Hand," which theological truth are they forgetting?

    A) That they should both try to be feet.

    B) That every part of the Body of Christ is important and has a special job to do.

    C) That hands are better than eyes.

    D) That they should stop being part of the body.

13. True or False: The Building is the Church If a church building burns down, the Church is gone.

In this level, we test your knowledge of the "Heart" and the "End."

14. The Emotion Alarm According to the "Theology of Emotions," what was **Anger** originally designed to do?

A) Make us feel powerful and scary.

B) Act as an "Alarm System" against things that are wrong and unjust.

C) Help us win arguments with our parents.

D) It was a mistake; God didn't mean to give us anger.

15. The "God-Centered" Happy If you are happy today because you are playing outside, what is the Junior Theologian's "move"?

A) To forget about God and just keep playing.

B) To "Trace" the joy back to the Giver and thank God for the happiness.

C) To feel guilty for being happy.

D) To ask for five more hours of playtime.

16. The Resurrection Hope When Jesus returns, what will happen to the bodies of those who trust Him?

A) They will stay in the ground forever.

B) They will be raised as "Glorified Bodies" that never get sick, old, or hurt.

C) They will turn into ghosts and fly on clouds.

D) They will look exactly the same as they do now.

17. The New Earth Mystery What is the "New Heavens and New Earth" going to be like?

A) A boring place where we just sing songs for a million years.

B) A renewed, perfect world where we live, work, and play with God face-to-face.

C) A place where there is no gravity.

D) It is just a dream; it isn't really going to happen.

In this final level, you must apply "Big Truths" to "Big Problems."

18. The "Secret Sin" Problem Imagine you did something wrong, and nobody—not your parents, your teachers, or your friends—saw you do it. Which attribute of God tells you that you should still confess it?

> A) God's Immutability.
>
> B) God's Omniscience (He knows everything).
>
> C) God's Beatitude (His happiness).
>
> D) God's Creation of the stars.

19. The "I'm Not Good Enough" Problem If you feel like God is mad at you because you failed a test or weren't "perfect," which doctrine reminds you that you are safe?

> A) The Doctrine of Justification (God already declared me "Not Guilty").
>
> B) The Doctrine of the Sun and Moon.
>
> C) The Doctrine of Fasting.
>
> D) The Doctrine of Church Buildings.

20. The "Unkind Neighbor" Problem If someone in your neighborhood is very mean and grumpy, why should you still treat them with respect?

> A) Because you want them to give you candy.
>
> B) Because they are an Image-Bearer of God, and God loves them.
>
> C) Because you are afraid of them.
>
> D) Because your mom told you to.

THE JUNIOR THEOLOGIAN'S ANSWER KEY & DEEP-DIVE EXPLANATION

(Read this section carefully! Even if you got the answer right, the "Why" is the most important part!)

Level 1 Answers: The Blueprint

1. Answer: B (God is Self-Existent/Aseity) Explanation: This is a huge building block of theology. Most things in the world need something else. A fire needs oxygen. A plant needs dirt. You need lunch. But God is the only "Uncaused Cause." He is the "I AM." He is the Boss of the universe because He is the only one who doesn't owe His life to anyone else. This should make us feel very safe! If God needed us, He might get tired of us. But since He doesn't need us, it means He loves us just because He *wants* to.

2. Answer: False Explanation: This is the doctrine of **Immutability**. In a world where your favorite toy breaks, your friends might move away, and your clothes get too small, God is the "Rock." He says in the Bible, "I the Lord do not change." His promises are like a contract that can never be broken. If He promised to love you in the Bible, He will never "change His mind" because you had a bad day.

3. Answer: 1-C, 2-D, 3-A, 4-B Explanation: * **Omniscience** (All-knowing) means God has the ultimate "Google" in His head.

- **Omnipotence** (All-powerful) means God's "batteries" never run out.

- **Omnipresence** (Everywhere) means God doesn't have a car because He's already where the car is going!

- **Immutability** (Unchanging) means God is the same yesterday, today, and forever.

4. Answer: B (Imago Dei) Explanation: This is the theology of "Human Value." Every single person, the kid who is hard to get along with, the person who looks different, and even your "enemy", is a masterpiece designed by God. When we are mean to people, we are actually being mean to God's artwork. A Junior Theologian sees the "hidden crown" on everyone's head.

5. Answer: C (Total Depravity) Explanation: This is the theology of "The Problem." We aren't just "kind of" messy; we are "Totally Depraved." This doesn't mean we are as bad as we could be (God's grace keeps us from that!), but it means sin is in our thoughts, our words, and our bodies. This is why we need a Savior, we can't just "try harder" to be good, we need a new heart!

6. Answer: B (100% God and 100% Man) Explanation: This is the **Hypostatic Union**. It is the most important math in the world! If Jesus were only God, He couldn't die for us. If He were only Man, His death wouldn't be powerful enough to save everyone. He had to be both to be the "Bridge" between Heaven and Earth.

7. Answer: C (The Prophet) Explanation: A **Prophet** is a messenger. In the old days, prophets said "Thus saith the Lord." But Jesus *is* the Lord. Everything He did and said was a message from God. When we read the Gospels, we are listening to the Ultimate Prophet tell us the secrets of the Kingdom.

8. Answer: B (Jesus is King) Explanation: This is the theology of **Sovereignty**. If your friend is in charge of the playground, you feel safe. If Jesus is in charge of the *entire universe*, you can feel even safer! Being a King means Jesus has the "final say" over your life, your school, and your future.

9. Answer: B (The Priest's Sacrifice) Explanation: In the Old Testament, the **Priest** stood between God and the people. He brought a lamb to pay for sins. Jesus is the "Great High Priest" because He didn't bring a lamb—He *was* the Lamb. He stood between us and God's justice and said, "Take Me instead." Now, He lives in Heaven and constantly prays for you!

10. Answer: B (The Great Exchange) Explanation: This is the heart of **Justification**. Imagine you have a bank account with a trillion dollars of "Debt" (Sin). Jesus has an account with a trillion dollars of "Credit" (Righteousness). On the Cross, He switched accounts with you. He took your debt and gave you His credit. Now, when God looks at your account, He sees Jesus' "Total."

11. Answer: B (Adoption Security) Explanation: This is the theology of **Family**. In ancient times, when you were adopted, it was a legal move that could never be undone. God didn't just "rescue" you like a lifeguard; He "adopted" you like a Father. You are a son or daughter of the King. Even when you mess up, you are still His child.

12. Answer: B (The Body of Christ) Explanation: This is **Ecclesiology**. The Church is a "Body." If you think you aren't important because you aren't a "pastor" or a "teacher," remember that a body needs its pinky toe just as much as its eyes! Every kid in the church has a job to do, even if it's just being the person who notices who is lonely.

13. Answer: False Explanation: The Church is a **People**, not a place. The "Invisible Church" is all believers everywhere. You could have church in a park, in a house, or in a basement. As long as the "called-out ones" are there, the Church is there!

Level 4 Answers: The Feelings & The Future

14. Answer: B (Anger as an Alarm) Explanation: This is the **Theology of Emotions**. God gets "Holy Anger" when He sees people being hurt. He gave us anger so we would want to protect people and stand up for what is right. The problem is our sin turns that "good anger" into "selfish anger." A Junior Theologian asks: "Is my alarm going off for God's reasons or my reasons?"

15. Answer: B (Gratitude/Tracing) Explanation: This is the theology of **Beatitude**. God is the source of all joy. When you are happy, don't stop at the "thing" (the toy or the game). Use that thing as a "ladder" to climb up and thank God. This makes your happiness last longer because it connects you to the King!

16. Answer: B (Glorified Bodies) Explanation: This is **Eschatology**. The Bible says our "lowly bodies" will be made like Jesus' "glorious body." Imagine your body, but with the "Upgrade" button pressed. No more glasses, no more braces, no more allergies, and no more getting tired! It's a physical resurrection.

17. Answer: B (The Renewed Earth) Explanation: Many people think Heaven is a boring cloud-city. But theology teaches us God is making a **New Earth**. We will have a world that is perfect—with mountains to climb, fruit to eat, and work to do—but without any of the bad stuff like thorns, sweat, or sadness. It's "Eden 2.0."

18. Answer: B (Omniscience) Explanation: This is the "Honesty Attribute." Since God already knows your secret, you aren't "hiding" it from Him, you're just hiding *yourself* from His grace. Confessing your sin is just saying "God, You saw that, and I'm sorry." It brings you back into the light.

19. Answer: A (Justification) Explanation: This is the "Peace Doctrine." If you feel like God is mad at you, remind yourself that He already "Judged" your sin at the Cross. He isn't a "cranky boss" waiting for you to fail; He is a "Loving Father" who has already declared you Righteous in Christ.

20. Answer: B (Image-Bearer) Explanation: This is the "Love Your Neighbor" doctrine. We don't love people because they are "nice." We love them because they belong to God. Treating a mean person with respect is a way of showing honor to the King who made them. It's like being nice to a Prince even if the Prince is having a bad day.

Final Score Review:

- **15-20 Correct: Master Theologian!** You have a solid grasp of the "System." You are ready to start teaching others how the Bible fits together. Keep studying and keep "Tracing" everything back to God!

- **10-14 Correct: Intermediate Theologian.** You have a great foundation, but some of the "Big Words" are still a bit tricky. Go back and read the "Action Manual" one more time to see how the doctrines fit into your daily life.

- **0-9 Correct: Apprentice Theologian.** You are just getting started! Don't be discouraged: theology is a life-long journey. Pick one attribute of God (like Love or Power) and focus on that for a week.

Conclusion of the Quiz: Theology isn't about being "smart"; it's about being "transformed." The reason we learn these things is so we can love God with all our **minds**. Now that you know the Blueprint, go out and live in the House!

PART 2: SYSTEMATIC THEOLOGY WORKBOOK FOR KIDS

Fun Bible Activities to Help Kids Understand God, Faith, and the Christian Life

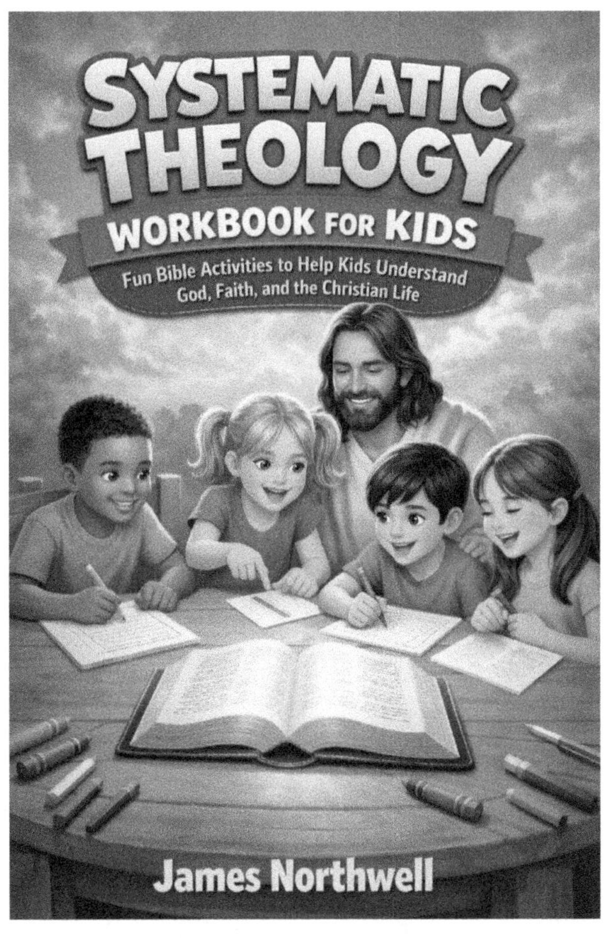

INTRODUCTION

GET READY TO KNOW GOD

Welcome to a very big adventure! You are about to start a project that is more exciting than building a giant LEGO castle or winning a soccer game. You are going to learn about the Person who made the stars, the oceans, and you.

The Bible tells us something amazing in **2 Peter 3:18**. It says, **"But grow in the grace and knowledge of our Lord and Savior Jesus Christ."** This means that God does not want to be a mystery to you. He wants you to know Him. He wants you to grasp how much He loves you and see the plan He has for the whole world.

This workbook is your guide to getting that knowledge. It is not a dry school book. It is a tool to help you see the big picture of faith. By the time you finish the last page, you will see how every story in the Bible fits together.

What is Systematic Theology?

That is a very long phrase, isn't it? Do not let the big words worry you. Let's break it down into two simple parts.

Theology simply means "the study of God." Every time you think about God or ask a question about the Bible, you are doing theology. If you wonder why God made the world or how Jesus could walk on water, you are a mini-theologian!

Systematic means "organized" or "put into a system." Think about your favorite grocery store. Imagine if the manager just threw all the food into one big pile in the middle of the store. You would find a gallon of milk sitting on top of a pile of hammers. You would find frozen pizza mixed in with the bananas. It would take you hours to find what you need.

A good store is systematic. It puts the fruit in one section and the cereal in another. This makes it easy for you to find exactly what you want. **Systematic Theology** does the same thing with the Bible. The Bible is a big book with 66 different parts. It has stories, poems, and letters. Sometimes, it is hard to find everything the Bible says about a specific topic, like angels or heaven.

This book takes those big topics and groups them together. We call these groups "doctrines." In each chapter, we will gather the pieces of the puzzle. When we put them together, we see a clear image of who God is.

Why Do We Need This Book?

You might wonder why you can't just read the Bible from start to finish. You should definitely do that! But the Bible is like a massive ocean. Sometimes, it helps to have a map so you know where the deepest parts are.

This workbook helps you build a solid foundation. Imagine building a house on a pile of sand. When the wind blows and the rain falls, the house will fall down. But if you build your house on a solid rock, it stays still. Learning these truths is like building your life on a rock. When you have hard questions or face tough times, you will know what is true. You won't have to guess what God thinks about you. You will know because you studied His Word.

How This Workbook Works

Each chapter in this book is like a new level in a game. You will learn a new truth and then use your brain and your hands to make it stick. Here is what you will find in every chapter:

- **The Focus Verse:** We start with one specific verse. This verse is the "key" to the whole lesson. I want you to read it out loud. Maybe even write it on a sticky note and put it on your mirror. This is a direct quote from God to you.

- **The Big Truth:** Here, we explain the topic. We use simple words to talk about things like creation, sin, and grace. We focus on the facts. We look at what the Bible says is true, no matter how we feel that day.

- **Action Activities:** This is the fun part! You will find crosswords, secret codes, and drawing challenges. We also included some "Home Labs." These are simple science experiments or crafts you can do with things in your kitchen. These activities help you see the truth in real life.

- **A Simple Prayer:** We end every chapter by talking to God. Knowing things about God is good, but knowing God as a friend is better. Prayer is how we build that friendship.

The Tools You Need

Before you turn to Chapter 1, let's make sure your workspace is ready. You do not need a lot of gear, but a few things will help:

1. **A Bible:** This is the most important tool. This workbook points to the Bible, but it does not replace it. Use a version that is easy for you to read. The ESV or NIrV are great choices for your age.

2. **Pencils and Colored Markers:** You will be doing a lot of drawing and writing. Use bright colors! God made a colorful world, so your workbook should be colorful too.

3. **A Curious Mind:** Do not be afraid to ask "Why?" or "How?" God is big enough to handle your questions. If you find something hard to grasp, ask a parent or a teacher to talk about it with you.

4. **A Little Time:** You do not have to rush. You could do one chapter a week. Take your time to think about the verses. Let the truths sink into your heart.

Is This Book for You?

If you are between 8 and 12 years old, this book was written just for you. But it is also great to share! You can work through these pages with a best friend or a sibling. You can even bring it to your Sunday School class.

Maybe you have been going to church your whole life. Or maybe you just picked up a Bible for the first time yesterday. It does not matter! This book starts at the very beginning. We will talk about how we got the Bible, who Jesus is, and what happens at the end of time.

A Quick Note to the Grown-Ups

If you are a parent or teacher reading this with a child, thank you! You are doing a great job. Your goal is to help your child see that the Bible is a cohesive story. It is not just a bunch of random rules. It is a story of a King who loves His people.

Feel free to help with the activities. Some of the "Home Labs" might need an extra pair of hands. Most importantly, listen to the questions your child asks. You don't always need to have the perfect answer. Just searching for the answer together in the Bible is a great way to bond.

Let's Start the Search

God is the Creator of everything. He is the King of kings. He is also a Father who loves His children. Getting to know Him is the best way to spend your time. When you know who God is, you start to know who you are, too.

You were made for a purpose. You were made to know God and enjoy Him forever. This book is just the start of that lifelong relationship.

Are you ready? Grab your favorite pen. Open your Bible. Let's look into the Word of God and see what He has to say to us!

CHAPTER 1

TRUST THE WORD OF GOD

Imagine you are camping in a deep, dark forest. The sun has gone down, and you cannot see your own hand in front of your face. You need to find your way back to your tent, but every tree looks the same. Suddenly, someone hands you a powerful flashlight. With one click, the path appears. You can see the rocks, the roots, and the trail. You are safe because you have light.

The Bible is that flashlight for your life. Without it, we would just be guessing about who God is. We would not know how we got here or where we are going. But God did not leave us in the dark. He gave us a book.

"Your word is a lamp for my feet, a light on my path." (Psalm 119:105)

Think about what a lamp does for your feet. It does not just show you the whole world at once. It shows you exactly where to step next. When you read the Bible, God shows you how to make good choices right now.

What is the Bible Exactly?

The Bible is not just one thick book. It is actually a library of 66 smaller books. It was written over a period of 1,600 years. That is a very long time! More than 40 different people wrote parts of it. Some were kings, some were fishermen, and one was even a doctor.

Even though many people wrote it, the Bible has only one main Author: God.

How does that work? The Bible explains this in a cool way. It says that all Scripture is "God-breathed." This does not mean God grew a pair of lungs and blew on the paper. It means His Spirit guided the writers. He made sure they wrote exactly what He wanted us to know. They used their own style and their own words, but the message came straight from God.

The Two Big Parts

The Bible is split into two main sections.

1. **The Old Testament:** This part was written before Jesus was born. It tells the story of how God made the world. It shows how He chose a special family (the Israelites) to show His love to the world. It is full of promises that a Savior was coming.

2. **The New Testament:** This part starts with the birth of Jesus. It tells us about His life, His death, and how He rose from the grave. It also tells us how the first churches started and how we can live for God today.

Both parts fit together like two pieces of a heart. You cannot have one without the other. The Old Testament promises the Savior, and the New Testament shows us who He is.

Some people say the Bible is just a book of fairy tales. But that is not true. There are three big reasons we can trust every word:

- **History Matches Up:** People who dig in the dirt (archaeologists) have found cities, coins, and buildings mentioned in the Bible. Every time they find something new, it proves the Bible was right about history.

- **Prophecies Come True:** A prophecy is when God tells someone what will happen in the future. The Bible has hundreds of these. For example, prophets said exactly where Jesus would be born hundreds of years before it happened. He was born in Bethlehem, just like they said.

- **It Changes Lives:** Millions of people have read this book and found hope. It helps people stop being mean and start being kind. It gives peace to people who are scared. A book of lies cannot change a human heart, but the Word of God can.

Activity 1: The Scripture Map

A map helps you get from Point A to Point B. In the space below (or on a piece of paper), draw a map of your own life.

1. Draw a "Start" line where you were born.
2. Draw a "Current Spot" where you are right now.
3. Add "Roadblocks" for things that are hard for you (like a tough subject in school or a fight with a friend).
4. Pick three Bible verses and write them next to the "Roadblocks."

For example, if you are scared, write: *"When I am afraid, I put my trust in you"* (Psalm 56:3). Now, look at your map. See how God's Word acts like a light on your path? It gives you a way through the hard parts!

Activity 2: The Bible Library Word Search

The Bible is a library full of special words. Can you find these six words in the list below? Write them down or see if you can spot them in your own Bible.

- **SCRIPTURE:** A fancy name for the holy words found in the Bible.

- **TESTAMENT:** This is a "Big Promise" God made to His people.

- **GOSPEL:** This means "Great News!" It tells us all about Jesus.

- **PROPHET:** A messenger God chose to share His words with others.

- **PSALM:** A song or a poem written to praise God.

- **AUTHOR:** The person who writes a story. God is the main Author of the Bible!

Home Lab: The Invisible Ink Message

God's Word is sometimes hidden in our hearts. Try this to see how "hidden" things can become clear.

What you need:

- A lemon or a little bit of milk
- A cotton swab (Q-tip)
- A white piece of paper
- A desk lamp (with a bulb that gets warm)

What to do:

1. Dip the swab into the lemon juice or milk.
2. Write your favorite Bible verse on the paper. It will look like nothing is there when it dries.

3. Hold the paper close to a warm light bulb (ask a parent for help!).

4. Watch as the heat makes the words appear!

The Lesson: Sometimes we don't understand the Bible right away. But when we spend time with God and let His "light" shine on the words, the meaning becomes clear.

How to Read Your Bible

You do not have to read 50 pages a day. Just start small. Here are three tips for your daily Bible time:

1. **Pick a Book:** Start with the Book of Mark in the New Testament. It is fast and full of action.

2. **Ask a Question:** After you read a few verses, ask: "What does this tell me about God?"

3. **Talk to God:** Tell Him what you learned. If you don't understand something, tell Him that too!

Talk to God

Dear God, thank You for giving me a flashlight for my life. Thank You for the Bible. Help me to trust what it says, even when I have big questions. Show me how to use Your Word to make good choices today. Amen.

CHAPTER 2

MEET THE ONE TRUE CREATOR

Have you ever spent an afternoon building something amazing with blocks or craft supplies? Maybe you built a tall tower or a colorful birdhouse. When you finished, you probably felt proud. You looked at your work and saw your own ideas come to life. You knew every piece of that project because you were the one who put it together.

The world is God's giant project. When we look at a tall mountain, a tiny ladybug, or the vast blue ocean, we are looking at God's handiwork. But God did more than just leave us a beautiful world to look at. He gave us His name. He told us His story. He wants you to know exactly who He is.

In this chapter, we are going to learn about the character of God. This is the foundation of everything else we believe. If we don't know who God is, we won't understand why He does what He does. Let's look at the amazing truth of our Creator.

"I am the Lord, and there is no other; apart from me there is no God. I will strengthen you, though you have not acknowledged me." (Isaiah 45:5)

This verse is like a royal decree. It tells us that God does not have any rivals. There are not many gods fighting for control of the weather or the stars. There is only one King. He is the only one who deserves our worship. He is the Boss of everything because He made everything. He is the first, the last, and the only True God.

Who is God?

Imagine trying to describe the entire ocean to a friend who has only ever seen a glass of water. It would be very hard, wouldn't it? You would talk about the waves, the deep trenches, and the millions of fish. Even then, your friend might not truly grasp how big the ocean is.

God is much bigger than our brains can fully understand. However, God does not want to be a total mystery to us. He tells us exactly who He is in the Bible. He uses special traits called **attributes**. Attributes are things that are always true about Him.

Humans change all the time. You might be happy one minute and grumpy the next. You grow taller every year. You learn new things and forget old ones. But God does not change. He does not have "bad days" where He is less kind or less powerful. He is the same yesterday, today, and forever.

The Six Great Truths About God

Let's look at six big things that make God who He is. These are the things that set Him apart from every person, every angel, and every creature.

1. God is Eternal

Everything you see had a beginning. You had a birthday. Your parents had a birthday. Even the trees, the rocks, and the sun had a start date. But God never had a start. He was always there before time began.

Think of a circle. If you put your finger on a circle and follow the line, you can never find the spot where it starts or ends. God is like that. He is the "Alpha and Omega," which are the first and last letters of the Greek alphabet. He has always existed, and He will always exist. This means He is never in a hurry and He never runs out of time.

2. God is All-Powerful (Omnipotent)

Have you ever tried to lift something that was just too heavy? We all have limits. We get tired, we get sick, and we run out of strength. God has no limits.

The Bible says that God spoke, and the stars appeared. He didn't need tools or a factory. He just used His powerful word. **Omnipotent** is a big word that means "all-powerful." There is no problem too big for God to solve. There is no enemy too strong for Him to defeat. When you feel small or weak, you can remember that your Father is the strongest force in the universe.

3. God is Everywhere (Omnipresent)

If you are at school, you cannot be at home at the same time. If you are in the living room, you aren't in the kitchen. We can only be in one place at a time. But God is everywhere at once.

He is with you while you read this book. He is also with a child on the other side of the planet at the exact same moment. He is at the bottom of the deepest ocean and on the highest mountain peak. This is wonderful news because it means you are never truly alone. You never have to go searching for God. He is always close enough to hear your quietest whisper.

4. God Knows Everything (Omniscient)

Think about the smartest person you know. Maybe it is a teacher or a scientist. Even they have to study and learn new things. God never has to learn. He already knows everything that has ever happened and everything that will happen.

He knows how many hairs are on your head. He knows the names of every star in the sky. He even knows what you are going to say before the words come out of your mouth! You never have to explain your feelings to God because He already sees them. He knows your heart better than you do, and He still loves you perfectly.

5. God is Holy

The word **holy** means that God is completely "set apart." He is perfect in every way. He never makes a mistake. He never thinks a mean thought. He never tells a lie.

Imagine a light so bright that it makes everything else look dim. That is like God's holiness. Because He is holy, He cannot be around sin. He is like a perfect judge who always does what is right and fair. Knowing God is holy helps us understand why we need Him to lead us. We want to follow the One who is always right.

6. God is Love

This might be the most famous thing about God. The Bible does not just say that God *acts* in a loving way. It says that **God is love**. Everything He does comes from His goodness.

Even when God gives us rules to follow, He does it because He loves us. Think about a parent who tells a child not to touch a hot stove. That rule is not there to be mean. It is there to protect the child. God's love is even bigger than that. He loves us so much that He wants to be with us forever.

How Can We See God?

Since we cannot see God with our eyes right now, how do we know He is there? God shows Himself to us in two main ways.

Nature: The Fingerprint of God When you look at a beautiful sunset, you see God's love for color and beauty. When you see a thunderstorm, you see His power. This is called "General Revelation." It is like finding a footprint in the sand. You might not see the person, but you know someone was there. Nature tells every person on earth that there is a powerful and creative God.

The Bible: The Voice of God Nature tells us that God is powerful, but it doesn't tell us His name. It doesn't tell us how to be saved or how much He loves us. For that, we need the Bible. This is called "Special Revelation." In the Bible, God speaks directly to us. He tells us His promises. He shows us His heart. While nature shows us His "fingerprint," the Bible shows us His "face."

To complete this hunt, you need to look around your house or your yard. Find an object that reminds you of one of God's traits. Write down what you found and why it reminds you of Him.

1. **Something Strong:** (Example: A heavy rock or a thick tree branch).
   o *I found:* _______________________________________
   o *Why:* ____

2. **Something Light:** (Example: A flashlight or a candle).
   o *I found:* _______________________________________
   o *Why:* ____

3. **Something Heart-Shaped:** (Example: A leaf or a drawing).
   o *I found:* _______________________________________
   o *Why:* ____

4. **Something Old:** (Example: An old photo or an antique book).
   o *I found:* _______________________________________
   o *Why:* ____

The Bible uses many special words to describe God. Can you find these six words in your heart or write them down?

- **ETERNAL:** God has no beginning and no end.

   ____

   ____

- **HOLY:** God is perfect and pure.

   ____

   ____

- **POWERFUL:** God can do anything.

   ____

   ____

- **LOVE:** God cares for us deeply.

    ____

    ____

- **PRESENT:** God is always with us.

    ____

    ____

- **CREATOR:** God made everything from nothing.

    ____

    ____

Home Lab: The Stained Glass Reminder

God's character is beautiful. It is like light shining through colored glass. Each color represents a different trait of God, but they all come from the same light.

What you need:

- Black construction paper
- Tissue paper (different colors)
- Scissors and glue
- A window with bright sunlight

What to do:

1. Draw a large shape on your black paper, like a cross or a star.
2. Carefully cut out the middle of the shape so you only have a black outline.
3. Cut small squares of colorful tissue paper.
4. Glue the tissue paper over the hole in your black paper. Use different colors for different attributes! Blue for power, red for love, white for holiness.
5. Tape your "stained glass" to a sunny window.

The Lesson: When the sun shines through the paper, the colors glow. This reminds us that when we get to know God, His light shines through our lives. People can see His love and kindness in the way we act!

While God is the King of the Universe, He also uses a very personal name. He invites us to call Him **Father**.

This is amazing! The same God who created the galaxies wants to have a relationship with you. A good father listens when his children talk. A good father protects his children from danger. A good father provides what his children need.

God is the perfect Father. Even if you have a great dad on earth, God is even better. If you don't have a dad around, God promises to be a Father to you. He is never too busy to listen to your prayers. He never gets tired of your questions. You are His child, and He delights in you.

Dear God, thank You for being the one true Creator. You are so much bigger and better than I can imagine. Thank You for being powerful enough to protect me and kind enough to love me. Thank You for being my Heavenly Father. Help me to trust You more every day as I learn about who You are. Amen.

CHAPTER 3

SEE GOD IN THREE PERSONS

Have you ever looked at a fidget spinner or a three-leaf clover? These are simple things that have three distinct parts but are still just one object. Today, we are going to look at the biggest mystery in the whole Bible. It is a concept that has made even the smartest people in history scratch their heads.

This mystery is called the **Trinity**.

The word "Trinity" is not actually in the Bible, but the idea is on almost every page. It describes how God is one God, but He exists in three distinct persons: the Father, the Son, and the Holy Spirit. If that sounds a bit confusing, do not worry! It is supposed to be big. If we could explain God as easily as a math problem, He wouldn't be God.

"Therefore go and make disciples of all nations, baptizing them in the name of the Father and of the Son and of the Holy Spirit," (Matthew 28:19)

Notice something very important in this verse. Jesus does not say to baptize them in the "names" (plural). He says in the "name" (singular). This is a huge clue! There is one name, one God, but three Persons mentioned. All three are equal, and all three have been together forever.

The Math of God

In your math class, you know that $1 + 1 + 1 = 3$. That is how the world works. But when we talk about God, the math looks a little different. It is more like $1 \times 1 \times 1 = 1$.

The Father is God.

The Son (Jesus) is God.

The Holy Spirit is God.

But there are not three gods. There is only one. Think of a musical chord. When a piano player hits three different notes at the same time, it makes one beautiful sound. You can hear the individual notes if you listen closely, but they work together to make one harmony. That is a small way to think about the Trinity.

1. God the Father: The Planner

When we think of God the Father, we often think of the Creator. He is the one who spoke the world into existence. He is like the great architect of a building. He drew the plans for the universe and knows exactly how everything should work.

The Father is the one who sent Jesus to earth because He loves us so much. He is also the one we talk to when we pray "Our Father, who art in heaven." He cares for us, protects us, and has a perfect plan for our lives. He is the source of all life and the King over all creation.

2. God the Son: The Savior

The Son is Jesus Christ. A common mistake is thinking that Jesus only started existing when He was born as a baby in Bethlehem. That is not true! Jesus has always existed with the Father. He was there when the stars were made.

Jesus is the "Word made flesh." This means He is the part of God we can see and touch. He came to earth to show us exactly what God is like. If you want to know how God feels about people who are hurting, look at Jesus. If you want to know how God feels about sin, look at Jesus.

Jesus did something no one else could do. Because He is 100% God and 100% man, He could be the bridge between us and the Father. He lived a perfect life and then took the punishment for our mistakes on the cross. He is our King, our Brother, and our best Friend.

3. God the Spirit: The Helper

The Holy Spirit is the third person of the Trinity. Sometimes people think of the Spirit as a "force" or a "ghost," but He is a Person. He has feelings, He speaks, and He helps us.

Before Jesus went back to heaven, He promised to send a Helper. That Helper is the Holy Spirit. Today, the Spirit lives inside everyone who trusts in Jesus. He is like a built-in compass. He helps us know right from wrong. He gives us the strength to be kind when we feel like being mean. He also helps us grasp the words we read in the Bible. He is God's presence with us every single day.

Seeing the Trinity in Action

One of the best places to see the Trinity is at the baptism of Jesus. Imagine you are standing by the Jordan River. You see Jesus (the Son) come out of the water. Suddenly, the sky opens up. The Holy Spirit comes down from heaven looking like a gentle dove and rests on Jesus. Then, a loud voice from heaven (the Father) says, "This is my beloved Son, in whom I am well pleased."

In that one moment, all three Persons of the Trinity were right there!

- **The Son** was in the water.
- **The Spirit** was descending like a dove.
- **The Father** was speaking from heaven.

They were working together to show the world that Jesus was starting His special mission.

Activity 1: The Three-in-One Science Lab

This experiment helps you see how one thing can be three things at the same time.

What you need:

- An adult to help you
- An ice cube
- A pot of water
- A stove

What to do:

1. **Solid:** Look at the ice cube. It is hard and cold. It is water (H_2O).
2. **Liquid:** Put the ice cube in the pot and turn on the heat. Soon, it melts. Now it is liquid. It looks different, but it is still water (H_2O).
3. **Gas:** Keep the water boiling. Look at the steam rising from the pot. That is water vapor. It is invisible and moves through the air. It is still water (H_2O).

The Lesson: Water can be ice, liquid, or steam. It is always the same substance, but it shows up in three different ways. This is a tiny bit like how God is Father, Son, and Spirit.

Activity 2: The Trinity Clover Hunt

Go outside and look for a three-leaf clover (or a shamrock). If you can't find one, you can draw one on a piece of paper.

1. On the first leaf, write **FATHER**.
2. On the second leaf, write **SON**.
3. On the third leaf, write **SPIRIT**.
4. In the center where the leaves meet, write **GOD**.

Now, try to pull one leaf off without touching the center. It is hard to do! The leaves are separate, but they are all part of the same plant. This is a famous way people have explained the Trinity for hundreds of years.

Why Does the Trinity Matter?

You might think, "This is cool, but does it change how I live?" Yes, it does! Here are three reasons why the Trinity is important for you:

1. God is never lonely. Because God is a Trinity, He has always been in a relationship. Before the world was made, the Father, Son, and Spirit loved each other. This means God didn't create you because He was bored or lonely. He created you because He has so much love that He wanted to share it with you!

2. We have a perfect example of teamwork. The Father, Son, and Spirit always work together. They never argue. They never try to show off. They show us how to treat our friends and family. When we work together with others, we are acting like God.

3. We are fully covered. The Father planned your life. The Son saved your life. The Spirit guides your life. Every part of God is working to help you know Him. You aren't just following a distant King; you are being cared for by a Team that loves you perfectly.

Activity 3: The Secret Code Message

Use the key below to find out what the Bible says about our relationship with the Trinity.

A=1, B=2, C=3, D=4, E=5, F=6, G=7, H=8, I=9,
L=12, O=15, S=19, T=20, U=21, V=22, W=23

"7 - 15 - 4" (___ ___ ___)

"9 - 19" (___ ___)

"12 - 15 - 22 - 5" (___ ___ ___ ___)

The Answer: "God is Love."

Wait, how does that relate to the Trinity? Because to have "love," you need someone to give love and someone to receive love. Because God is three Persons, He has been loving for all of eternity!

"Is Jesus just a junior version of God?"

No way! Jesus is just as much God as the Father is. He has all the power and all the holiness of God. He just has a different role.

"If Jesus is God, who was He talking to when He prayed?"

This is a great question. When Jesus was on earth, He talked to God the Father. This shows us that the three Persons of the Trinity really are distinct. They can talk to each other and love each other.

"Can I see the Holy Spirit?"

Not with your eyes. The Bible compares the Spirit to the wind. You cannot see the wind, but you can see what the wind *does*. You can see the leaves move on a tree. In the same way, you can see the Spirit by the way He changes people's hearts and makes them more like Jesus.

Home Lab: The Trinity Pretzel

This is a tasty way to remember the lesson!

What you need:

- Pretzel dough or store-bought soft pretzels
- Salt
- A baking sheet

What to do:

1. Take a long piece of dough and roll it into a snake.
2. Cross the ends over to make three distinct loops that all join in the middle.
3. Bake them and enjoy!

The Lesson: As you eat your pretzel, look at the three loops. Each loop is separate, but they are all made of the same dough. They are joined together to make one snack. This is a reminder of our one God in three Persons.

Dear God, thank You for being so big that I cannot fully grasp everything about You. Thank You, Father, for making me. Thank You, Jesus, for saving me. Thank You, Holy Spirit, for being my Helper. I am glad that I can know You and that You are always with me. Help me to show Your love to others today. Amen.

CHAPTER 4

EXPLORE THE WORLD GOD MADE

Have you ever walked outside on a clear night and looked up at the stars? It feels like looking at a giant, sparkling blanket. Or have you ever watched a tiny ant carry a crumb three times its size? When we look at the world, we are seeing a masterpiece. Every mountain, every whale, and every atom was put there on purpose.

In the first three chapters, we learned about the Bible and who God is. Now, we are going to look at the first thing God did in the Bible. He created. He went from being the only thing that existed to being the King of a massive, colorful universe.

The Focus Verse

**"In the beginning God created the heavens and the earth."
(Genesis 1:1)**

This is the very first sentence of the Bible. It is short, but it tells us a lot. It tells us that time has a "start." It tells us that God was already there before the start. And it tells us that everything we see, the "heavens and the earth", belongs to Him because He made it.

The Big Start: Out of Nothing

When you build a birdhouse, you need wood, nails, and a hammer. You take things that already exist and put them together. God did something different. He created "ex nihilo." That is a Latin phrase that means "out of nothing."

Before God started, there was no dirt. There was no air. There was no light. There was only God. Then, God spoke. He didn't use a magic wand or a construction crew. His words have so much strength that when He said, "Let there be light," light appeared instantly.

The Seven Days of Creation

God is a God of order. He didn't just throw everything into a pile. He built the world like a beautiful house, room by room. Let's look at how He did it.

Day 1: Light and Dark

God created light. He separated the light from the darkness. This gave us day and night. Think about how fast light travels. It moves at 186,000 miles per second! God made that entire system with just one sentence.

Day 2: The Sky and Water

God made the atmosphere. He separated the water on the earth from the clouds in the sky. He gave us air to breathe and a beautiful blue sky to look at.

Day 3: Land and Plants

God told the water to move aside so dry land could appear. Then, He decorated the land. He made grass, trees, flowers, and fruit. He didn't just make one type of plant; He made thousands! He made prickly cacti, giant redwood trees, and sweet strawberries.

Day 4: Sun, Moon, and Stars

Wait a minute! God made light on Day 1, but He made the sun on Day 4? Yes! This shows that God is the source of all light. On Day 4, He put "lights" in the sky to help us track time, seasons, and years. The sun gives us warmth, the moon guides the tides, and the stars show us how vast God's imagination is.

Day 5: Birds and Fish

The sky and the oceans were ready for life. God made creatures to fly through the air and swim through the deep. He made the tiny hummingbird and the massive blue whale on the same day. He told them to fill the earth with even more life.

Day 6: Land Animals and Humans

This was a very busy day! God made lions, elephants, dogs, and bugs. But then, He did something extra special. He made humans. We will talk more about this in the next chapter, but for now, remember that humans are the "crown" of creation. We were made to rule over the earth and take care of it.

Day 7: Rest

Did God get tired? No! Remember, God never runs out of energy. He rested to show us a pattern. He stopped to enjoy what He had made. He looked at everything and said it was "very good."

Why Did God Create the World?

God didn't create the world because He was bored. He didn't need us to keep Him company. He created the world for two big reasons.

1. To Show His Glory The world is like a giant sign pointing to God. The thunder shows His power. The sunset shows His beauty. The way your body heals a paper cut shows His wisdom. Every part of nature says, "Look how amazing my Creator is!"

2. To Share His Love God is full of joy. He wanted to create beings who could enjoy the world with Him. He wanted us to see the stars and feel the wind and know that He is good. Creation is a gift from God to us.

In the sections below (or on a separate paper), Draw a small icon or symbol for each day of creation. Use the list above to help you.

- **Day 1:** (Maybe a sunbeam or a candle)

- **Day 2:** (Maybe a cloud or a wave)

- **Day 3:** (Maybe a flower or a mountain)

- **Day 4:** (Maybe a crescent moon and stars)

- **Day 5:** (Maybe a bird wing or a fish tail)

- **Day 6:** (Maybe a paw print or a person)

- **Day 7:** (Maybe a pillow or a smiley face)

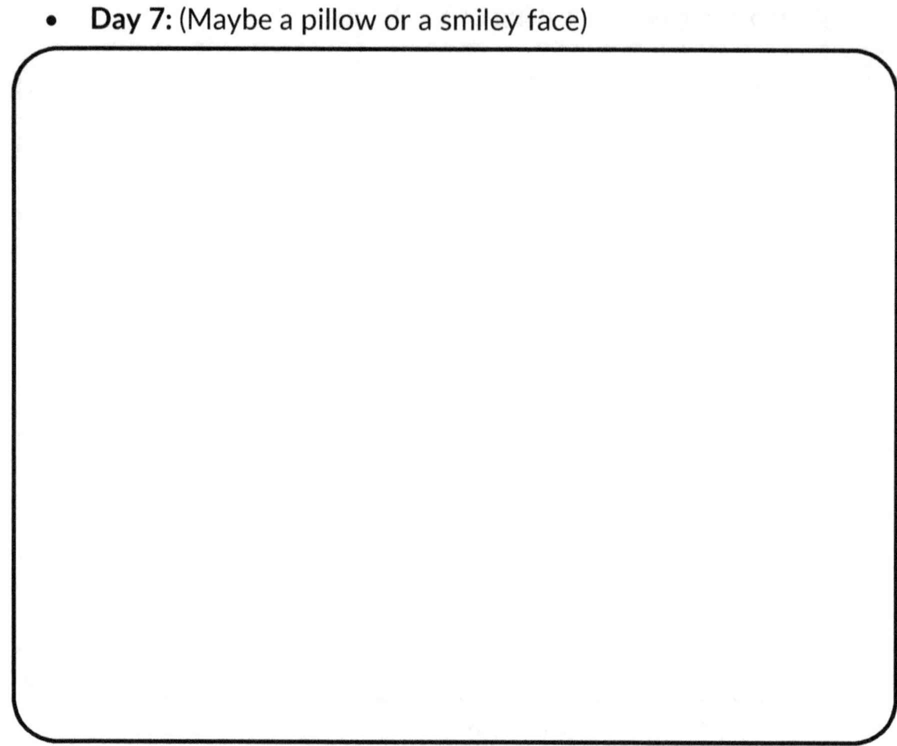

Once you finish, look at your calendar. Which day is your favorite? Why do you think God chose that specific order?

Activity 2: The Seven Days of Art

God used words to create, but He also used color and shape. You are an artist too! Pick one "Day" from the list. Get a piece of paper and use markers, paint, or crayons to make the most detailed version of that day you can imagine.

If you pick **Day 5**, don't just draw one fish. Draw a coral reef with neon fish, a shark, and a jellyfish! If you pick **Day 3**, draw a forest with different types of leaves. When you finish, show your art to someone and tell them what God created on that day.

Taking Care of the House

Since God made the world and gave it to us, we have a job to do. This job is called **stewardship**. A steward is someone who takes care of something that belongs to someone else.

Imagine your friend lets you borrow their favorite video game. You wouldn't throw it in the mud or break the case, right? You would keep it safe because it belongs to your friend. The earth belongs to God, but He let us "borrow" it.

We can be good stewards by:

- Not wasting water or food.
- Taking care of animals.
- Not littering in the park.
- Thanking God for the beautiful things we see.

Home Lab: The "Breath of Life" Seed Experiment

God gave plants the ability to grow from tiny seeds. You can watch this happen in your own kitchen!

What you need:

- A clear plastic bag
- A paper towel
- A few dried beans (like lima beans or kidney beans)
- A little water

What to do:

1. Wet the paper towel so it is damp but not dripping.
2. Fold the towel and put it inside the plastic bag.
3. Place the beans on top of the paper towel.
4. Seal the bag and tape it to a sunny window.
5. Check it every day for a week.

The Lesson: Within a few days, you will see a tiny sprout come out of the bean. This is the "life" God put inside every plant on Day 3. Even a tiny bean has a plan inside it! It knows exactly how to become a big plant because God designed it that way.

Common Questions About Creation

"How long was a 'day' in Genesis?" Some people think it was exactly 24 hours. Others think it might have been a long period of time. The most important thing is that God did it! He is the one who designed the system and made it work.

"What about dinosaurs?" The Bible says God made all the land animals on Day 6. That would include the big ones like the T-Rex and the tiny ones like lizards! God made every creature, even the ones that aren't around anymore.

Dear God, thank You for this incredible world. Thank You for the bright sun, the green grass, and the funny animals You made. When I look at creation, help me to remember how powerful and creative You are. Help me to be a good steward of the earth You gave us. Amen.

CHAPTER 5

KNOW YOU ARE MADE IN GOD'S IMAGE

In the last chapter, we saw how God made the sun, the stars, and the blue whales. Those things are all massive and beautiful. But did you know that God saved His best work for last? On the very same day He made the lions and the elephants, He made something even better. He made people.

You might think a galaxy is more impressive than a person because it is so big. Or you might think a cheetah is cooler because it can run so fast. But in God's eyes, you are the most precious thing in the entire universe. You are not just another animal. You are a special creation made to look like the King.

**"So God created mankind in his own image, in the image of
God he created them; male and female he created them."
(Genesis 1:27)**

This verse uses a very special phrase: **"the image of God."** In Latin, this is called the *Imago Dei*. It means that God built a little bit of His own character into every single human being. You are like a mirror that is meant to reflect the light of God to the rest of the world.

What Does "In His Image" Mean?

Does God have two arms, two legs, and a nose like you? Not exactly. The Bible tells us that God is Spirit. Being made in His image does not mean we look like Him on the outside. It means we are like Him on the inside.

God gave us traits that animals do not have. These traits allow us to talk to God and act like Him. Let's look at four ways you carry the image of God right now.

1. You Are Creative

God is the Great Creator. He made the world out of nothing. Because you are made in His image, you love to create things too! Think about the last time you drew a picture, built a fort, or wrote a story. You were using your imagination. Birds build nests and beavers build dams, but they always do it the same way. Only humans make art, music, and movies. When you create, you are reflecting the God who made the stars.

2. You Know Right from Wrong

Have you ever felt a "tugging" in your heart when you did something mean? That is your conscience. God is perfectly holy and just. He put a sense of "rightness" inside of you. A lion does not feel guilty after it hunts. It is just being a lion. But you know that being kind is better than being mean. You know that telling the truth is better than lying. This moral compass is a gift from God.

3. You Can Use Language

God spoke the world into existence. He is a God who communicates. He gave you the ability to use words to express your feelings and ideas. You can pray to God. You can tell your parents you love them. You can read a book and learn about the past. No other creature can use language to share complex thoughts the way humans do.

4. You Can Have Relationships

In Chapter 3, we learned that God is a Trinity. The Father, Son, and Holy Spirit have always loved each other. Since you are made in God's image, you were made for friendship too. You feel a need to belong to a family and have friends. We are happiest when we are loving others and being loved by them. This is because God is love, and He made us to be like Him.

The Big Difference: Humans vs. Animals

Sometimes people say that humans are just "smart animals." But the Bible says something different. While we should be kind to animals, they are not made in God's image.

Imagine a beautiful statue of a famous King. The statue is not the King, but it represents him. If someone spray-paints the statue, they are insulting the King. People are God's "statues" on earth. We represent Him. This is why every single person deserves respect. It doesn't matter how old they are, what they look like, or where they come from. Every person carries the thumbprint of God on their soul.

Activity 1: The Mirror Reflection Challenge

Go stand in front of a mirror. Look closely at your reflection. Now, answer these questions on a piece of paper or in your head.

1. **List three physical things about yourself:** (Example: I have brown eyes, I am tall, I have curly hair).

    ----

2. **List three "image" traits about yourself:** (Example: I am good at math, I like to help people, I love to sing).

\--

\--

\--

\--

\--

3. **Think of a way you used your words today to help someone.**

\--

\--

\--

\--

\--

4. **Think of something you created this week.**

\--

\--

\--

\--

\--

The Lesson: The things in List 1 are your physical body. The things in List 2 and 3 are your *Imago Dei*. They are the parts of you that are like God! When you look in the mirror, don't just see your hair or your skin. See a person who was made to reflect the King of the Universe.

You Are Not an Accident

Some people think the world happened by chance. They think humans are just a lucky mistake. But the Bible says that God knit you together in your mother's womb (Psalm 139:13).

God chose your eye color. He chose your personality. He knew exactly what day you would be born. You are not a mistake. You are a masterpiece. Even if you feel like you aren't good at sports or school, you are still valuable. Your value does not come from what you *do*. Your value comes from *whose* you are. You belong to God.

God is like a Master Designer. He put "secret codes" of His own character inside of you. Use the **Secret Key** below to solve the four "Image Traits" that God gave you.

The Secret Key: 1=A, 2=E, 3=I, 4=O, 5=U (Every number is a vowel!)

1. CR __ __ T __ V __ (Code: 2 − 1 − 3 − 2) *This means you can make art, music, and new things!*

2. L __ V __ NG (Code: 4 − 3) *This means you can care for people with all your heart.*

3. SP __ __ K __ R (Code: 2 − 1 − 2) *This means you use words to share big ideas and truth.*

4. J __ ST (Code: 5) *This means you want things to be fair and right.*

Activity 3: The "One-of-a-Kind" Design

God didn't use a cookie cutter when He made people. He made everyone different! In the space below, create a "Profile Card" for yourself to celebrate how God made you.

- **My Name:**

- **One thing I am really good at:**

- **My favorite way to be creative:**

- **A person I can show God's love to this week:**

The Big Takeaway: You don't have to be "perfect" to reflect God. A cracked mirror can still reflect the sun! Even though we make mistakes, we still have great value because of who made us.

Home Lab: The Unique Fingerprint Art

God made you so unique that even your fingerprints are different from everyone else who has ever lived. There are billions of people on earth, but no one has your exact prints!

What you need:

- An ink pad (or a washable marker)
- White paper
- A magnifying glass (if you have one)

What to do:

1. Press your thumb onto the ink pad or color it with a washable marker.
2. Press your thumb firmly onto the white paper.
3. Do this for all ten of your fingers.
4. Use a magnifying glass to look at the tiny swirls and lines.
5. Now, use your markers to turn your fingerprints into little characters! Draw hats, legs, and arms on them.

The Lesson: Every one of those tiny lines was designed by God. He is a God of detail. If He cares enough to make your fingerprints unique, imagine how much He cares about your thoughts, your dreams, and your heart!

How Should We Treat Others?

If every person is made in God's image, how should we treat the people we meet?

- **The kid at school who is lonely:** Since they are made in God's image, they are royalty! We should show them kindness.
- **The person who is different from us:** Different skin colors or languages are just different ways God shows His creativity. We should celebrate the variety.

- **The person who is mean to us:** Even they carry God's image, though it might be "dusty" or broken by sin. We should still treat them with the respect that God's image deserves.

When we are mean to others, we are actually being disrespectful to the God who made them. When we love others, we are showing love to God.

Body and Soul

There is one more thing that makes humans special. We are made of two parts. We have a **Body** (the part you can see) and a **Soul** (the part you can't see).

Your body is like a house, and your soul is the person living inside. Your soul is the part of you that thinks, feels, and will live forever. When God made the first man, Adam, He breathed life into him. That breath made him a "living soul." Animals have the breath of life, but only humans have a soul that can know God. This is why we can pray and feel God's presence.

Talk to God

Dear God, thank You for making me in Your image. Thank You for giving me a mind to think, a heart to love, and a voice to praise You. Help me to remember how valuable I am to You. Help me to see Your image in every person I meet today. Teach me to treat others with the respect and kindness they deserve. Amen.

CHAPTER 6

FACE THE PROBLEM OF SIN

Have you ever tried to fix something that was broken? Maybe you dropped a favorite ceramic mug and it shattered into a dozen pieces. Even if you use the best glue in the world, you can still see the tiny cracks. The mug is still a mug, but it isn't "perfect" anymore.

In the last chapter, we learned that people are made in the image of God. We are like that beautiful mug. But something happened that caused a giant crack in that image. That "something" is what the Bible calls sin. To understand the rest of the Bible story, we have to look at how things got broken and why we cannot fix them on our own.

"For all have sinned and fall short of the glory of God."
(Romans 3:23)

This verse is very direct. It does not say "some" people or "bad" people have sinned. It says **all**. Imagine a high jump competition where the bar is set as high as the clouds. No matter how fast you run or how high you jump, you will always fall short of reaching it. That is what sin does. It keeps us from reaching God's perfect standard.

What Exactly is Sin?

Sin is a word we use a lot in church, but what does it mean? In the original language of the Bible, one of the words for sin comes from archery. It means **"to miss the mark."** Imagine an archer aiming for a bullseye. If the arrow hits the dirt or flies over the target, the archer missed the mark. God's "bullseye" is perfect holiness. When we do things our way instead of God's way, we miss the mark.

Sin shows up in three main ways:

1. **Doing what is wrong:** Like telling a lie or taking something that isn't yours.
2. **Not doing what is right:** Like seeing someone get bullied and staying silent instead of helping.
3. **The "I" Problem:** This is the root of sin. It is wanting to be our own boss instead of letting God be the King.

The Story of the First Crack

How did this start? It goes back to the very first two people, Adam and Eve. God put them in a perfect garden. They had everything they needed. God gave them only one rule: do not eat from the Tree of the Knowledge of Good and Evil. He gave them this rule because He loved them and wanted to protect them.

But a serpent came and whispered lies. He told them that God was holding out on them. He suggested that if they ate the fruit, they could be like God. Adam and Eve chose to believe the lie. They ate the fruit.

That one act of disobedience changed everything. It was like a drop of black ink falling into a glass of pure water. The ink spread to every part of the water. Because Adam and Eve were the heads of the human family, that "ink" of sin spread to every person born after them.

The Results of the Fall

When Adam and Eve sinned, the world "fell" away from its perfect state. This is why we call it **The Fall**. It brought three big "breaks" into the world:

- **The Break with God:** Before sin, Adam and Eve walked with God in the garden. After sin, they were afraid and tried to hide. Sin creates a giant canyon between us and God. Because God is holy, He cannot be near sin.

- **The Break with Each Other:** Have you noticed how easy it is to argue with your siblings? After the Fall, Adam blamed Eve, and Eve blamed the serpent. Sin makes us selfish, which hurts our relationships.

- **The Break with Creation:** This is why we have weeds in gardens, natural disasters, and sickness. The world is "groaning" because sin messed up the balance of nature.

Activity 1: The "Broken Image" Puzzle

Find an old cereal box or a piece of cardboard. On the plain side, draw a picture of a person (you!). Decorate it with bright colors.

1. Now, use scissors to cut the picture into 10 messy, jagged pieces.
2. Mix them up on the floor.
3. Try to put the puzzle back together.

The Lesson: You can put the pieces back in the right spot, but the lines where the paper was cut are still there. You can't make the paper "one piece" again just by pushing them together. This is like us. We are still God's masterpieces, but we are "broken" by sin. We need a Master Maker to make us new.

Imagine you are standing on one side of a deep, rocky canyon. On your side, it is dark and lonely. On the other side, it is bright, beautiful, and God is there. You want to get to the other side, but there is no bridge.

In the Bible, our "good works" are like trying to build a bridge. We might try to use wood (being kind) or stones (going to church) or rope (obeying rules). But no matter how hard we try, our bridge is always too short to reach the other side.

Fill in the blanks below to see why we can't cross the gap on our own:

1. **THE GAP:** The name of the big canyon that keeps us away from God is called

    S __ __. (Hint: It rhymes with "pin").

2. **THE JUMP:** If the canyon is 100 feet wide and you jump 10 feet, do you make it? (Yes or No).

3. **THE TRUTH:** Even if you are the "best" kid in the world, can you be as perfect as God? (Yes or No).

The Lesson: We cannot build a bridge to God by being "good enough." We need someone from the other side to come and rescue us.

Is There Any Good News?

Reading about sin can feel a bit sad. It's a big problem! But we have to understand the bad news so we can truly love the Good News.

If you didn't know you were sick, you wouldn't go to the doctor. If you didn't know the house was on fire, you wouldn't call for help. Understanding sin helps us realize that we need a Savior.

The Bible says that while we were still sinners, God already had a plan to fix the "cracks." He didn't leave us in the dark forest. He didn't leave us on the other side of the canyon. He decided to build a bridge. We will learn all about that bridge in the next few chapters!

Sin starts small, but it gets very heavy.

What you need:

- A backpack
- Several heavy books or rocks

What to do:

1. Put on the empty backpack. Walk around the room. It feels light and easy, right?
2. Now, have someone add one heavy book. This represents a "small" sin, like a tiny lie. Walk again.
3. Add five more books. These represent more sins—disobeying parents, being mean, putting yourself first.
4. Try to run or jump with the full backpack.

The Lesson: Sin is a burden. It slows us down and makes us tired. It keeps us from being the joyful, free people God made us to be. Only Jesus can take that backpack off our shoulders and give us rest.

Activity 3: Clear the Vowels

God wants to wash us clean. Below are some words about sin, but the vowels (A, E, I, O, U) have been replaced by a "scrum" of ink. Can you figure out the words?

1. **G __ __ L T** (The feeling we have when we do wrong)
2. **H __ D __ NG** (What Adam and Eve did in the garden)
3. **PR __ D __** (Thinking we are better than others)
4. **L __ __ S** (Words that are not true)

Answers: 1. GUILT, 2. HIDING, 3. PRIDE, 4. LIES

Talk to God

Dear God, I know that I have missed the mark. I have done things my own way instead of Your way. Thank You for showing me the truth about sin so that I can see how much I need You. Thank You that You don't leave me alone in my mistakes. Help me to be honest about my sin and look to You for help. Amen.

CHAPTER 7

MEET JESUS, THE PROMISED SAVIOR

If you have ever played a game of hide-and-seek, you know the feeling of being "found." In the last chapter, we saw how sin made Adam and Eve want to hide from God. But God didn't want them to stay hidden. He didn't want the "crack" in the world to stay broken forever.

Immediately after the Fall, God made a promise. He promised that one day, a Savior would come to crush the power of sin and death. Thousands of years went by, and God kept dropping clues through the prophets about who this Savior would be. Finally, in a small stable in Bethlehem, the Promise arrived.

"She will give birth to a son, and you are to give him the name Jesus, because he will save his people from their sins."
(Matthew 1:21)

The name **Jesus** actually means "The Lord Saves." It wasn't just a popular name back then; it was His job description! Jesus didn't come to earth just to be a good teacher or a famous leader. He came for a specific mission: to be the bridge across the gap of sin.

Who is Jesus? (The Two Truths)

To understand Jesus, you have to hold two big ideas in your head at the same time. This is called the **Hypostatic Union** (that's a giant phrase to impress your parents with!). It simply means:

1. **Jesus is 100% God:** He is the Son of God. He has always existed. He has all the power and holiness of God because He *is* God.

2. **Jesus is 100% Man:** He was born as a baby. He grew up, He got hungry, He got tired, and He felt pain. He had a human heart and a human brain.

Why does this matter? Because to bridge the gap between God and humans, the Savior had to belong to both sides! He had to be a man so He could represent us, and He had to be God so He could be perfect enough to pay for our sins.

The Perfect Life

Think back to the "Archery" example from Chapter 6. Everyone else who has ever lived has "missed the mark." We have all sinned. But Jesus lived for about 33 years and **never once missed.**

- He never told a lie to get out of trouble.

- He never had a selfish thought.

- He always obeyed His parents and His Heavenly Father.

- He always loved people perfectly, even the ones who were mean to Him.

Because Jesus was perfect, He was the only person in history who didn't deserve to be punished for sin. This is what made Him the perfect "Substitute."

The Three Offices of Jesus

In the Old Testament, God used three types of people to lead His people. Jesus came to be the "Ultimate" version of all three:

- **The Prophet:** A prophet brings God's Word to the people. Jesus didn't just *bring* the Word; He *is* the Word. He taught us exactly how God wants us to live.

- **The Priest:** A priest stands between God and people to offer sacrifices. Jesus didn't just *offer* a sacrifice; He *was* the sacrifice. He is our way to talk to God.

- **The King:** A king rules over his kingdom. Jesus is the King of kings. He rules with love and kindness, and His kingdom will never end.

Activity 1: The "Who is Jesus?" Fill-in-the-Blank

Use the words in the **Word Bank** to complete the sentences about Jesus.

Word Bank: *Bridge, Perfect, Savior, God, Man*

1. Jesus is fully __________ and fully __________.
2. Because Jesus never sinned, His life was __________.
3. Jesus is the __________ that connects us back to God.
4. The name "Jesus" means the Lord is our __________.

Activity 2: The Prophet, Priest, and King Roles

Jesus has three main "jobs" or titles. Fill in the missing letters to name them!

1. **PR__PH__T:** He teaches us God's Word and tells us the truth.
2. **PR__ __ST:** He stands between us and God to help us be friends with Him.
3. **K__NG:** He is the boss of the whole universe and rules with love.

The Greatest Rescue Mission

Imagine you are trapped in a deep, dark pit. You try to climb out, but the walls are too slippery. A teacher walks by and shouts, "You should have been more careful!" A philosopher walks by and says, "Just imagine you aren't in a pit."

But then, Jesus comes by. He doesn't just give you advice from the top. He climbs down into the pit with you, puts you on His shoulders, and carries you out.

That is what the "Incarnation" (God becoming human) is all about. Jesus left the perfect beauty of heaven to come into our messy, sinful world. He did it because He loves you and didn't want to be in heaven without you.

Home Lab: The "Weight Lifter" Demonstration

Remember the backpack full of books from Chapter 6? Let's see what Jesus does with that weight.

What you need:

- The heavy backpack (from the Chapter 6 Home Lab)
- A strong volunteer (like a parent or older sibling)

What to do:

1. Put on the heavy backpack. Try to do five jumping jacks. It's hard!
2. Now, have your volunteer stand behind you and lift the bottom of the backpack while you jump.
3. Finally, take the backpack off and give it to the volunteer. Let them wear it while you run around.

The Lesson: Jesus saw that the weight of our sin was too heavy for us to carry. He didn't just help us lift it; He took it from us completely. He carried the weight of the whole world's sin so that we could be free and "light."

Activity 3: The Name Above All Names

Below, write the name **JESUS** in big, bold letters. Decorate it with things that represent His roles:

- Draw a small **Crown** over the "J" (for King).
- Draw a small **Cross** in the "S" (for Savior).
- Draw a small **Scroll** or Book under the "U" (for Teacher/Prophet).

Jesus being born and living a perfect life was the first half of the rescue. But there was a debt that had to be paid. In the next chapter, we are going to look at the most important Friday in history, the day Jesus gave everything to bring us home.

Talk to God

Dear Jesus, thank You for coming to earth for me. Thank You for being the perfect Bridge between me and God. I am amazed that You are the King of the universe, yet You care about my life. Help me to learn from Your teachings and follow You as my King. Amen.

CHAPTER 8

ACCEPT THE GIFT OF GRACE

Imagine it is your birthday. You wake up early, race to the living room, and see a box sitting on the table. It is wrapped in the shiny, golden paper you love, topped with a massive, curly red bow. Your name is written on the tag in big, bold letters.

You didn't build this gift. You didn't work a job to pay for it. You didn't even have to clean your room perfectly to "deserve" it. Your parents bought it because they love you. To make it yours, you only have to do one thing: reach out, pull the ribbon, and open the box.

In the last chapter, we saw the incredible price Jesus paid on the Cross. He did the hard work. He paid the "bill" for our sin. Now, He stands before you with a gift in His hands. That gift is called **Grace**. In this chapter, we are going to explore exactly what Grace is, why it is so different from everything else in the world, and how you can officially open it.

"For the wages of sin is death, but the gift of God is eternal life in Christ Jesus our Lord." (Romans 6:23)

This verse explains the "Great Exchange" perfectly. A **wage** is something you earn. If you do chores for an hour and get five dollars, that is your wage. Because of our sin, the "wage" we earned was to be separated from God. But the second half of the verse is the Good News! It says that life with God isn't a wage we earn, it is a **free gift**. Gifts aren't earned; they are simply received with a thankful heart.

What Exactly is Grace?

The word "Grace" is one of the most important words in the entire Bible. To understand it, we have to compare it to two other words: **Justice** and **Mercy**.

1. Justice (Getting what you deserve)

Imagine you accidentally broke a neighbor's window while playing ball. Justice means you have to pay to fix the window. You did the damage, so you pay the price. In our life with God, Justice would mean we stay separated from Him because of our sin.

2. Mercy (NOT getting what you deserve)

Imagine your neighbor sees the broken window, looks at you, and says, "I know you're sorry. I'm not going to make you pay for it. I forgive you." That is Mercy. It's when the punishment we earned is taken away.

3. Grace (Getting what you DON'T deserve)

Now, imagine the neighbor not only forgives you for the window but also invites you inside, gives you a giant slice of chocolate cake, and hands you a brand-new, better baseball. That is **Grace**! It is God giving us His love, His friendship, and a home in Heaven, even though we didn't do anything to earn it.

The Story of the Two Builders

Let's imagine two people trying to reach a beautiful island in the middle of a vast sea.

Builder A thinks he can get there by working hard. He starts swimming as fast as he can. He swims for hours, but the island is hundreds of miles away. No matter how hard he tries, he gets tired and realizes he will never be strong enough to make it on his own. He is trying to reach God through "works."

Builder B knows he can't swim that far. He stands on the shore and waits. Suddenly, a massive, beautiful ship pulls up. The Captain leans over the side and says, "I have already sailed to the island and back. I have plenty of room. Do you want to come with me for free?"

Following Jesus is like getting on the ship. The "Ship of Grace" carries us where we could never go on our own.

Activity 1: Reflections on Grace

In the space below, answer these three questions in your own words.

1. Think of a time you were given a gift you didn't expect. How did it feel to receive it without having to "work" for it?

   ----

2. Why do you think God chose to make salvation a **gift** instead of something we have to earn?

   ----

3. Based on what we learned about "Justice" and "Grace," what is the biggest difference between the two?

Even though a gift is free, it doesn't do you any good if it just sits on the table. If your friend offers you a piece of candy, it doesn't become yours until you reach out your hand and take it.

In the Bible, **Faith** is the "hand" that reaches out to take the gift of Grace. Faith isn't just a feeling; it is **trust**.

The ABCs of Faith

We often use these three letters to help us remember how to reach out and take God's gift:

- **A – Admit:** You admit that you have sinned. You tell God, "I know I can't reach the 'island' by swimming on my own. I need Your help."

- **B – Believe:** You believe that Jesus is the Son of God and that His death on the cross paid for your sins. You trust that the "Ship" is strong enough to carry you.

- **C – Choose:** You choose to let Jesus be the King of your life. You decide to step onto the ship and go where He leads.

The Great Swap

When you accept the gift of Grace, something amazing happens that the Bible calls "Justification." It sounds like a big legal word, but it just means "Just-as-if-I'd" never sinned.

Imagine you are wearing a white t-shirt that is covered in mud, grass stains, and ink. That represents our sin. Now imagine Jesus is wearing a robe that is perfectly white, glowing, and clean.

Grace is when Jesus walks up to you and says, "Let's trade." He takes your stained shirt and puts it on Himself. Then, He takes His perfect, clean robe and puts it on you. Now, when God looks at you, He doesn't see the "mud" of your mistakes. He sees the "white robe" of Jesus!

Faith really just means **Trust**. Think about these everyday examples of faith:

- When you sit in a chair, you have "faith" that it won't break.
- When you turn on a faucet, you have "faith" that water will come out.

In the space below, write down three other things you "trust" every single day:

1. ____
2. ____
3. ____

The Big Point: Salvation is putting that same kind of trust in Jesus. You are "sitting down" on His promise that He has saved you.

Home Lab: The "Penny and the Vinegar" Clean-Up

This experiment shows that we can't make ourselves clean, but a "solution" from the outside can!

What you need:

- A few very old, dirty, brown pennies.
- A small bowl of vinegar mixed with a spoonful of salt.
- A paper towel.

What to do:

1. Look at the pennies. They are covered in "oxidation" (the dark brown stuff). You can't rub it off with your fingers.
2. Drop the pennies into the vinegar and salt. Count to 20.
3. Take them out and rinse them with water.

The Lesson: The pennies didn't "work hard" to get shiny. They just had to be "submerged" in the solution. When we "immerse" ourselves in God's grace, He washes away the old, dirty parts of our character and makes us shine like new!

"Do I have to be 'extra good' after I get the gift?" You don't do good things to *get* the gift, but you will *want* to do good things because you are so thankful for the gift! Imagine someone saved your life—you would want to be their best friend and help them however you could, right? That is why we follow God's rules—out of love, not out of fear.

"What if I make a mistake tomorrow?" Grace doesn't run out. If you mess up, you don't lose the gift. You just go back to God, tell Him you're sorry, and He helps you get back on track. His Grace is new every single morning.

Talk to God

If you want to accept this gift today, or if you just want to thank God for it, you can talk to Him right now:

"Dear God, thank You for the Gift of Grace. I admit that I have sinned and I can't fix it on my own. I believe that Jesus died for me and rose again to pay my debt. Today, I choose to take Your hand and follow You. Thank You for loving me even when I make mistakes. Help me to live a life that shows how thankful I am for Your gift. Amen."

CHAPTER 9

WALK WITH THE HOLY SPIRIT

Have you ever tried to find your way through a thick forest at night? Or maybe you've tried to put together a 1,000-piece puzzle without the picture on the box? It is hard to do things alone when you don't have a guide or a helper.

In the last chapter, we learned about the amazing gift of Grace. When you accept that gift, God doesn't just give you a "ticket to heaven" and then leave you to figure the rest of your life out by yourself. He gives you a Helper. That Helper is the **Holy Spirit**. In this chapter, we are going to learn who the Holy Spirit is and how He helps us walk through life every single day.

**"But the Advocate, the Holy Spirit, whom the Father will
send in my name, will teach you all things and will remind
you of everything I have said to you." (John 14:26)**

Before Jesus went back to heaven, He promised His friends that He wouldn't leave them as orphans. He promised to send the Holy Spirit. Think about that: the same God who created the stars and the same Jesus who walked on water now lives **inside** of you through the Holy Spirit. You never have to go anywhere alone again!

Who is the Holy Spirit?

Sometimes people get confused about the Holy Spirit. He isn't a "ghost" like you see in movies, and He isn't just a "feeling." The Holy Spirit is **God**. Remember back in Chapter 3 when we talked about the Trinity? The Holy Spirit is the third Person of the Trinity.

Because He is God, He is powerful, wise, and kind. When you become a Christian, the Holy Spirit comes to live in your heart. This is called "Indwelling." He becomes your constant companion.

The Three Jobs of the Holy Spirit

The Holy Spirit is very busy! He has several special jobs He does in your life:

1. The Comforter

In the Bible, one of the names for the Holy Spirit is "Paraclete," which means "one who walks alongside." When you are sad, lonely, or scared, the Holy Spirit provides a peace that doesn't make sense to the rest of the world. He reminds you that God loves you and that you are safe.

2. The Teacher

Have you ever read a Bible verse and thought, *"I have no idea what this means"*? That is when you can ask the Holy Spirit for help! He is the one who wrote the Bible (through human authors), so He is the best teacher in the world. He helps the "lights go on" in your brain so you can understand God's truth.

3. The Compass

A compass tells a traveler which way is North so they don't get lost. The Holy Spirit acts like a spiritual compass. He "convicts" us, which is a church word for a "nudge" in our heart, when we are about to do something wrong. He also guides us toward the right choices, like being kind to a new student or telling the truth even when it's hard.

Activity 1: The Helper's Roles

Based on what you just read, think about your own life. Write down a time when you might need the Holy Spirit to do one of these jobs for you.

- **I need the Comforter when:**

- **I need the Teacher when:**

- **I need the Compass when:**

The Fruit of the Spirit

How can you tell if the Holy Spirit is really working in someone? You look at their "fruit." Just like an apple tree produces apples, a person who "walks with the Spirit" produces certain qualities.

The Bible says the **Fruit of the Spirit** is Love, Joy, Peace, Patience, Kindness, Goodness, Faithfulness, Gentleness, and Self-Control (Galatians 5:22-23).

Notice that the Bible says "fruit" (singular), not "fruits" (plural). It's like a bunch of grapes; they all grow together! You can't grow these by trying really hard to be "good." Instead, as you spend time with the Holy Spirit,

He grows them in you. You might notice that you are suddenly more patient with your siblings or more joyful even when things go wrong. That's the Holy Spirit at work!

Activity 2: Fruit Check-In

Look at the nine Fruits of the Spirit listed above.

1. Which fruit do you see growing in your life right now? Give an example.

----

2. Which fruit do you want the Holy Spirit to help you grow more of?

How Do We "Walk" with the Spirit?

"Walking with the Spirit" just means staying in step with Him. Imagine you are walking with a friend. If you run way ahead, you can't hear them. If you stop and sit down, they leave you behind. To walk with them, you have to stay close and listen.

We stay close to the Spirit by:

- **Listening:** When you feel that "nudge" in your heart to do something good, do it!
- **Asking:** Start your day by saying, "Holy Spirit, help me to follow You today."
- **Filling Up:** Spend time in the Bible so the Spirit has God's Word to use to guide you.

The Bible often compares the Holy Spirit to the wind. You can't see the wind, but you can see what it **does**.

What you need:

- A small paper boat (or a toy boat).
- A tub of water.
- Your own breath (or a small fan).

What to do:

1. Put the boat in the water. It just sits there, right? It has no power to move on its own.
2. Now, blow gently on the sail. Watch the boat move across the water.
3. Try blowing from different directions.

The Lesson: We are like the boat. On our own, we don't have the power to live a "God-sized" life. But the Holy Spirit is like the wind. When we "set our sails" toward Him, He provides the power to move us in the right direction. He does the work; we just have to catch the wind!

Talk to God

"Dear Holy Spirit, thank You for being my Helper. Thank You for living in my heart and promising never to leave me. Please be my Teacher when I read the Bible and my Compass when I have to make hard choices. Grow Your fruit in my life so that others can see Jesus in me. Amen."

CHAPTER 10

JOIN THE FAMILY OF GOD

Imagine for a moment that you are standing outside a grand, beautiful house during a rainstorm. Inside, you can see a large family sitting around a fireplace. They are laughing, sharing a meal, and telling stories. There is a sense of warmth and safety in that room that you can feel even through the window. You want to go inside, but you aren't sure if you belong. Then, the front door swings wide open, and the Father of the house stands there with a smile. He doesn't ask for your ID card, and he doesn't ask if you've worked hard enough to earn a seat at the table. He simply says, "Welcome home. You're part of the family now."

In our previous chapters, we learned about the incredible **Grace** of God and how the **Holy Spirit** comes to live within us as our Helper. But being a Christian isn't just a "me and God" thing. When you accept the gift of salvation, you aren't just rescued; you are **adopted**. You have been brought into a massive, worldwide, eternal family. In this chapter, we are going to explore what it means to be a child of God, how we treat our new brothers and sisters, and the amazing organization God created to keep us together: **The Church.**

"See what great love the Father has lavished on us, that we should be called children of God! And that is what we are! The reason the world does not know us is that it did not know him." (1 John 3:1)

Notice that the Bible doesn't say God "gave" us a little bit of love. It says He **lavished** it on us. To lavish something means to pour it out in huge, overflowing amounts, like pouring a whole gallon of chocolate syrup on one scoop of ice cream! God didn't just forgive your sins; He went much further. He changed your status. You went from being a stranger to being a son or a daughter of the King of the Universe.

What is Adoption?

In the world we live in, adoption happens when a family chooses a child to be their very own. They sign legal papers that say, "This child is now ours. They have our name. They have a right to everything we own. They are just as much a part of this family as if they were born into it."

The Bible says that is exactly what God did for you.

- **He Chose You:** God didn't wait for you to find Him; He sought you out.

- **He Gave You His Name:** We are called "Christians" because we carry the name of Christ.

- **He Shares His Inheritance:** Everything that belongs to Jesus, peace, joy, and eternal life, now belongs to you, too.

The Worldwide Family

Because God is your Father, every other person who trusts in Jesus is your brother or sister. This family is bigger than any sports team fan base or any country. It includes people who speak languages you've never heard, people who eat foods you've never tasted, and people who lived hundreds of years before you were even born!

When you meet another Christian, even if they live on the other side of the planet, you have something in common that is stronger than anything else: you share the same Father.

Activity 1: My Family Traits

When people are in the same family, they often look alike. Spiritual family members have "traits" too! Based on what we've learned, what are three things that should show up in the lives of God's children?

1. ____

2. ____

3. ____

What is "The Church"?

When many people hear the word "church," they think of a building with a steeple, some stained glass, and wooden benches. While those buildings are nice, they aren't actually the Church.

The Church is the People. The word used in the Bible for church is *ekklesia*, which means "a gathered assembly." It's like a giant team huddle. The building is just the locker room where the team meets to get instructions from the Coach (God) before going out to play the game (living for God in the world).

The Body of Christ

The Bible uses a very cool metaphor to explain how the Church works. It says the Church is like a **human body**.

- **Jesus is the Head:** He is the brain that tells the body what to do.

- **We are the Parts:** Some of us are hands, some are feet, some are ears, and some are eyes.

Think about how your own body works. Your hand is great at picking things up, but it can't hear a song. Your ear is great at hearing music, but it can't walk to the kitchen. For the body to work, every part has to do its job, and every part has to stay connected to the head.

If you decide you don't need the Church, it's like a finger trying to live all by itself on a table. It won't work! We need each other to be healthy.

Every person in God's family has been given a "gift" or a "talent" to help the rest of the family. Look at the list below and circle the ones you think you might be good at:

- **Encouraging:** Saying kind words to someone who is sad.
- **Serving:** Helping clean up or setting up for an event.
- **Giving:** Sharing your things or money with people in need.
- **Teaching:** Explaining Bible stories to younger kids.
- **Leading:** Helping organize a group to get a task done.
- **Listening:** Being a good friend to someone who needs to talk.

How can you use one of these "parts" this week to help your church family?

The "One Anothers"

Because we are family, God gave us specific instructions on how to treat each other. In the New Testament, there are over 50 "one another" commands. Here are a few of the most important ones:

1. **Love one another:** This is the big one! Jesus said people would know we follow Him by how much we love our church family.

2. **Forgive one another:** Families have disagreements. Sometimes brothers and sisters are mean or selfish. But because God forgave us, we have to be quick to forgive each other.

3. **Carry one another's burdens:** If a family member is going through a hard time, maybe they are sick or sad, the rest of the family steps in to help carry the weight.

4. **Pray for one another:** We talk to our Father about the needs of our brothers and sisters.

Sometimes, on a rainy Sunday morning, it might feel easier to stay in bed and watch cartoons. But gathering with the family of God is like charging a battery. When you go to church, three important things happen:

- **Instruction:** You learn more about God's Word so you can grow strong.
- **Worship:** You join your voice with others to tell God how great He is. There is something powerful about singing with hundreds of other people!
- **Fellowship:** You spend time with friends who believe what you believe. They remind you that you aren't alone in following Jesus.

Home Lab: The "Coal and the Fire" Demonstration

This shows why staying connected to the Church family is so important for your faith.

What you need:

- A parent or adult to help you (this involves a grill or a fireplace).
- A pile of charcoal or wood.

What to do:

1. Look at a pile of burning coals in a grill. When they are all bunched together, they stay red-hot and create a lot of heat.
2. Have an adult use tongs to take one single coal out of the pile and move it to the far corner of the grill, all by itself.
3. Watch what happens to that one coal over the next few minutes.

The Lesson: The coal that was moved away from the others will quickly turn grey and lose its heat. It didn't "stop being coal," but it lost its fire. We are just like those coals. When we stay close to other Christians, our "fire" for God stays hot. If we try to do it all alone, our faith can get cold and grey. We need the "heat" of our church family!

Activity 3: The Family Portrait

In the space below, draw a picture of your "Church Family." It doesn't have to be everyone in the building! Draw your Sunday school teacher, your pastor, or the friends you play with at church.

Write one reason you are thankful for the people in your drawing:

What If the Church Isn't Perfect?

Have you ever had a fight with your brother or sister? Of course! Even though we are God's family, we are still people who make mistakes. Sometimes people in the church are mean, or they say things that hurt our feelings.

When that happens, remember this: the Church is not a museum for perfect people; it is a **hospital** for people who are healing. We are all "under construction." Just because a family member makes a mistake doesn't mean they aren't your family anymore. We stay, we forgive, and we help each other grow.

Talk to God

"Dear Father, thank You for adopting me into Your family. It is amazing to know that I am Your child and that I have brothers and sisters all over the world. Thank You for my church and for the people who help me learn about You. Help me to be a good 'part of the body' and to use my gifts to help others. Teach me how to love and forgive my church family just like You love and forgive me. Amen."

CHAPTER 11

TALK WITH YOUR HEAVENLY FATHER

Imagine for a moment that you found a secret, golden telephone hidden in a drawer in your room. This isn't a normal phone; it doesn't need a charger, it never loses its signal, and it only has one number saved in it. If you pick up that phone, the person on the other end is the King of the Universe. He isn't too busy to talk. He doesn't put you on hold. He doesn't have an assistant tell you to "call back later." The moment you whisper a word, He is listening with 100% of His attention.

In the last chapter, we learned that you are now a part of God's family. One of the greatest privileges of being a child of God is that you have a direct line to your Father. We call this **Prayer**.

Many people think prayer is a scary, formal thing that you only do in church while wearing fancy clothes and using old-fashioned words. But the truth is much more exciting. Prayer is simply **talking to God**. It is a conversation between a child and a Father who loves them more than anything. In this chapter, we are going to learn how to talk to God, what to say, and how to listen for His voice.

The Focus Verse

"Do not be anxious about anything, but in every situation, by prayer and petition, with thanksgiving, present your requests to God." (Philippians 4:6)

Notice the words **"in everything."** God doesn't just want to hear about the "big" stuff, like when someone is sick or when you have a big test. He wants to hear about the small stuff, too! He wants to know about the cool bug you found, the joke that made you laugh, and the thing that made you feel a little bit lonely at lunch. If it matters to you, it matters to Him.

How Do We Pray?

Some kids worry that they don't know the "right" words to say. They think if they don't say "Amen" at the right time or use big words, God won't hear them. But remember, God is your Father. Does a dad care if his toddler uses perfect grammar when they say, "I love you"? Of course not! He just loves hearing their voice.

You can pray:

- **Out loud or in your head:** God hears your thoughts just as clearly as your words.

- **With your eyes open or closed:** Closing your eyes just helps you focus, but you can pray while walking to school or riding your bike!

- **Anywhere and anytime:** You don't have to be in a church building. You can pray in bed, on the playground, or in the middle of a crowded room.

The P.R.A.Y. Method

If you aren't sure where to start, you can use the word **P.R.A.Y.** to help you remember four great things to talk to God about:

P – Praise (Adoration)

Start by telling God how great He is. This isn't for His benefit (He already knows He's great!), it's for ours. It helps us remember how big and powerful our Father is.

- *Example: "God, You are so creative! Thank You for making the mountains and the oceans."*

R – Repent (Confession)

This is where we are honest about our mistakes. We tell God we are sorry for the times we "missed the mark" today. Because of Grace, we don't have to be afraid to tell Him the truth.

- *Example: "Father, I'm sorry I was mean to my sister this morning. Please help me to be kind."*

A – Ask (Petition)

This is where we tell God what we need. It's okay to ask for things! We can ask for help for ourselves and for other people.

- *Example: "Please help my Grandma feel better, and help me not to be nervous about my math test."*

Y – Yield (Thanksgiving)

To yield means to say, "I trust Your plan more than mine." We thank Him for what He has already done and tell Him we trust Him with the future.

- *Example: "Thank You for my family. I trust You to lead me today. Your way is the best way."*

Activity 1: My P.R.A.Y. Journal

Use the space below to write a short prayer using the four steps we just learned.

- P (Praise): ____
- R (Repent): ____
- A (Ask): ____
- Y (Yield/Thank): ____

This is a big question. Sometimes we pray for something—like a sick pet to get better—and it doesn't happen the way we wanted. Does that mean God didn't hear us? No. God always answers, but He answers like a wise Father, not a vending machine.

Think of it this way. A Father can say three things:

1. **YES:** "I love that idea! Here it is."
2. **NO:** "I love you too much to give you that, because I know it will hurt you or it isn't what's best."
3. **WAIT:** "Not yet. I have something better planned, but you have to trust Me and be patient."

God sees the "whole picture" of your life. We only see one small piece of the puzzle. When God says "No" or "Wait," it's because He loves us, not because He isn't listening.

The Model Prayer: The Lord's Prayer

One day, Jesus' disciples asked Him, "Lord, teach us to pray." Jesus gave them a beautiful example that we still use today. It's called **The Lord's Prayer**.

In this prayer, Jesus shows us that we should start by honoring God's name, asking for His Kingdom to come on earth, and asking for our "daily bread" (the things we need to get through the day). He also reminds us to ask for forgiveness and to ask for protection from temptation.

Activity 2: Daily Bread Check-In

What are three things you need "daily bread" for today? It could be patience, energy, food, or a brave heart.

1. ____

2. ____

3. ____

If you went to a friend's house and talked for an hour without letting them say a single word, would that be a very good conversation? Probably not! Prayer is a two-way street. We talk to God, but we also have to **listen** to Him.

How does God "talk" back?

- **Through His Word:** Most of the time, God answers our prayers through the verses we read in the Bible.

- **Through the Holy Spirit:** As we learned in Chapter 9, the Spirit gives us "nudges" or quiet thoughts in our hearts.

- **Through Other People:** Sometimes a parent or teacher says exactly what we needed to hear.

- **Through Circumstances:** Sometimes God opens or closes a door to show us which way to go.

Home Lab: The "Cup Phone" Experiment

This experiment shows how communication works and how we need to stay "connected" to hear clearly.

What you need:

- Two paper cups.
- A long piece of string (about 10–15 feet).
- A paperclip or tape.

What to do:

1. Poke a small hole in the bottom of each cup.
2. Thread the string through the holes and tie a knot (or use a paperclip) to keep the string from pulling out.
3. Give one cup to a partner and walk away until the string is **tight**.
4. Whisper into your cup while your partner holds theirs to their ear.

The Lesson: If the string is loose or floppy, the sound won't travel. You can't hear anything! But when the string is pulled tight, the connection is clear. Prayer is our "string" to God. When we stay focused and "tight" in our relationship with Him, we can hear His heart more clearly.

One of the most powerful things you can do is pray for someone else. This is called **Intercession**.

Who can you pray for today?

- **A Family Member:** ___________________________________
- **A Friend:** ___________________________________
- **A Teacher or Leader:** _______________________________
- **Someone who is hurting:** _____________________________

"Dear Heavenly Father, thank You that I don't need a special phone or a fancy building to talk to You. Thank You for listening to me every time I pray. Help me to remember to talk to You about everything, the big things and the small things. Teach me how to listen for Your voice in my heart and in Your Word. I am so glad that You are my Father. Amen."

CHAPTER 12

LIVE A LIFE FOR GOD'S GLORY

Have you ever seen a mirror in a dark room? If there is no light, the mirror doesn't look like much. It's just a dark, cold piece of glass. But the moment you turn on a lamp or open the curtains to let the sun in, something amazing happens. The mirror begins to shine! It looks like there is a light *inside* the mirror, but we know the truth: the mirror is simply reflecting the light from somewhere else.

This is the secret to living a life for **God's Glory**. In the previous chapters, we learned how to talk to God, how to walk with the Spirit, and how to belong to His family. Now, we ask the big question: *"What am I supposed to do with my life?"*

The answer is simpler than you might think. You are called to be God's mirror. You aren't the source of the light, but you are designed to reflect His beauty, His kindness, and His love to everyone around you. Living for God's glory means making Him look as great to others as He truly is.

"So whether you eat or drink or whatever you do, do it all for the glory of God." (1 Corinthians 10:31)

Did you catch that? Even the smallest, most normal things, like eating a sandwich or drinking a glass of water, can be done for God's glory. You don't have to be a preacher on a stage or a missionary in a jungle to glorify God. You can glorify Him in your classroom, on the soccer field, while doing your chores, or while playing with your friends.

What Does "Glory" Actually Mean?

"Glory" is a big church word, but in the Bible, it often carries the idea of **weight** or **importance**. To glorify God means to show the world that He is the most important thing in your life.

Imagine you have a backpack. If you fill it with feathers, it's light and unimportant. But if you fill it with gold bricks, it becomes heavy and valuable. When we glorify God, we are telling the world, "God isn't a 'feather' in my life; He is the 'gold.' He is the most valuable person I know."

The Three Ways We Reflect God's Glory:

1. **Our Words:** How we speak to our parents, our teachers, and even people who are mean to us.
2. **Our Actions:** The choices we make when no one is watching.
3. **Our Attitude:** Having a heart of thankfulness instead of complaining.

Activity 1: The Glory Spotlight

Imagine you are a stage director and you have a giant spotlight. You can point it at yourself to make everyone look at you, or you can point it at God to make everyone look at Him.

In the situations below, how can you "turn the spotlight" toward God?

- **Situation 1:** You just won a trophy for being the best player on your team.

- o *Instead of saying "I'm the best," you could say:*

- **Situation 2:** You see a student at school sitting all alone and crying.

  - o *To show God's kindness, you could:*

- **Situation 3:** Your mom asks you to clean your room when you really want to play video games.

  - o *To glorify God with your attitude, you could:*

The "Salt and Light" Mission

Jesus gave us two very cool nicknames to help us understand our mission in the world. He called us the **Salt of the Earth** and the **Light of the World**.

1. You are the Salt

Have you ever eaten a french fry without salt? It's a bit bland, right? Salt does two things: it adds flavor and it preserves things (keeps them from rotting). As a Christian, your life should "add flavor" to the world. You should be the person who brings joy, peace, and kindness into a room. You also "preserve" the world by standing up for what is right when others are doing what is wrong.

2. You are the Light

Light does one main thing: it chases away the dark. In a world that can sometimes be dark with sadness, anger, or lies, your life should be a bright spot. You don't have to be a giant bonfire; even a tiny candle can help someone find their way in a dark room.

Think about your "world": your home, your school, and your neighborhood. Where is one "dark" spot where you could bring some light this week? (Maybe a lonely neighbor, a messy park, or a friend who is sad).

My Plan to Shine: "This week, I will ______________________________

because I want to ______________________________________

show God's glory to ____________________________________

One of the best ways to glorify God is by **serving**. Jesus is the King of Kings, but when He was on earth, He did something shocking. He put on a towel and washed His disciples' dirty, dusty feet. He showed us that the greatest people in God's Kingdom are the ones who help others.

Serving isn't always about big projects. It's about having "servant eyes." This means looking around and asking, *"Who needs help right now?"* * It's picking up a piece of trash that isn't yours.

- It's letting someone else go first in line.
- It's helping your teacher move chairs without being asked.

When you serve others, people often ask, "Why are you being so nice?" That is your chance to tell them, "Because God has been so good to me!"

This experiment shows how we need to stay close to the Light to reflect the Light.

What you need:

- Something that "glows in the dark" (like a plastic star or a glow-stick).
- A very bright lamp or a sunny window.
- A dark closet.

What to do:

1. Take your glow-in-the-dark object into the dark closet. It probably doesn't glow very much.

2. Now, hold the object right up against a bright light bulb for 60 seconds. (Be careful not to touch the hot bulb!)

3. Immediately go back into the dark closet.

The Lesson: The object glows because it "soaked up" the light from the lamp. It can't glow on its own. If you want your life to "glow" with God's glory, you have to spend time close to Him in prayer and in His Word. The closer you stay to the Light, the brighter you will shine!

Living for an Audience of One

Sometimes we try to do good things because we want people to clap for us or tell us how great we are. But if we do that, we are glorifying ourselves, not God.

Living for God's glory means living for an **"Audience of One."** This means that even if no one else sees you do the right thing, you are happy because you know God sees you.

- If you find a dollar on the floor and turn it in to the teacher, and no one ever finds out it was you, God saw it, and He is glorified.

- If you work really hard on your homework even when you're tired, God saw it, and He is glorified.

When we live for Him, we don't need the world to clap. We are waiting for the day when we hear Him say, *"Well done, good and faithful servant."*

Activity 3: The Glory Log

For the next 24 hours, try to keep a "Glory Log." Every time you do something, no matter how small, with the goal of making God look good, write it down here.

Talk to God

"Dear Heavenly Father, thank You for the privilege of being Your mirror. I want my life to show the world how wonderful, kind, and powerful You are. Help me to have 'servant eyes' so I can see who needs help today. Whether I am playing, studying, or helping at home, help me to do it all for Your glory. Let my light shine so that others will see my good works and praise You. Amen."

CHAPTER 13

LOOK FORWARD TO A NEW HOME

Have you ever been on a long car ride to a place you really love? Maybe it's a trip to a theme park, your grandparent's house, or the beach. The car ride might be bumpy, you might get tired of sitting still, and you might even ask, "Are we there yet?" a dozen times. But the whole time you are in the car, you have a smile on your face because you know where you are going. The destination makes the journey worth it.

Our life on earth is a lot like that car ride. In the last twelve chapters, we have learned how to know God, how to follow Jesus, and how to live for His glory right now. But the story of the Bible doesn't end on earth. God has promised us a final destination that is more beautiful, more fun, and more peaceful than anything we can imagine. He is preparing a **New Home** for us.

"He will wipe every tear from their eyes. There will be no more death or mourning or crying or pain, for the old order of things has passed away." (Revelation 21:4)

Think about your favorite day ever. Now, imagine a place where *every* day is even better than that one. In our New Home, all the "sad things" from Chapter 6 will be gone forever. No more boo-boos, no more mean words, no more getting sick, and no more saying goodbye. Everything that sin broke, God is going to fix.

What is Heaven Like?

People often ask, "Will I be bored in heaven? Will I just sit on a cloud and play a harp all day?" The answer is a big, loud **NO!** The Bible describes our future home as a "New Heaven and a New Earth." It won't be a floaty, ghostly place. It will be a real world with mountains, trees, water, and cities, except it will be perfect.

The Five "No-Mores" of the New Home:

1. **No More Darkness:** God's glory will be so bright we won't even need a sun or a moon.
2. **No More Fear:** You will feel 100% safe, 100% of the time.
3. **No More Sin:** No one will ever be mean, selfish, or dishonest again.
4. **No More Sadness:** Every "broken heart" will be totally healed.
5. **No More Separation:** We will be with God, seeing Him face-to-face!

Activity 1: The "Everything New" List

If you could pick three things from this world that you think God might make "even better" in the New Earth, what would they be? (Example: Puppies that never get old, fruit that tastes like candy, or being able to run without getting tired).

1. ____
2. ____
3. ____

The Great Reunion

The best part of a new home isn't the gold streets or the beautiful gates; it's the **people**.

When we get to our New Home, we will be reunited with all our brothers and sisters in Christ who have gone there before us. You'll get to meet David (the giant-slayer), Esther (the brave queen), and Peter (the fisherman). You will get to hear their stories in person!

But most importantly, you will be with **Jesus**. All the things we talked about in this book, His love, His grace, His power, you will get to experience while standing right next to Him. He is the one who built the home, and He is the one who makes it "Heaven."

Activity 2: A Letter to Future Me

Imagine you are already in the New Home, and you are looking back at the life you are living right now. What would you want to tell yourself about why it was worth it to follow Jesus?

*"Dear Me, Don't give up when things are hard, because _________

Being here with Jesus is ___________________________________

Living with "Heaven Eyes"

Knowing that we have a perfect home waiting for us changes how we live today. It gives us **Hope**.

When a runner is in a race and their legs start to hurt, they don't stop. They look at the finish line and keep going. When you have a hard day at school or when things feel unfair, you can look at the "finish line" of Heaven.

- You can be **generous** today because you know you have riches waiting in Heaven.

- You can be **brave** today because you know God has already won the victory.

- You can be **patient** today because you know the "car ride" is almost over.

Home Lab: The "Telescope" Focus

This experiment shows how focusing on the future changes how we see the present.

What you need:

- A cardboard tube (from a paper towel roll).

- A small toy or picture placed at the other end of a long hallway.

What to do:

1. Look down the hallway normally. You can see the toy, but you also see the walls, the floor, the ceiling, and maybe some clutter.

2. Now, put the tube to your eye like a telescope and look *only* at the toy.

3. Everything else (the clutter and the walls) disappears from your view.

The Lesson: When we focus only on our problems (the clutter), we get overwhelmed. But when we use the "telescope" of faith to look at our New Home and the promise of Jesus, the problems don't seem so big anymore. We are focused on the prize!

Activity 3: The Welcome Home Drawing

The Bible says that in the New City, there is a "River of the Water of Life" and the "Tree of Life" with leaves that heal the nations. Draw a picture of what you think the entrance to your New Home might look like.

Write your favorite word to describe Heaven here:

Talk to God

"Dear Jesus, thank You for preparing a place for me. When I feel sad or scared, help me to remember that this world is not my final home. Thank You that one day there will be no more tears and no more pain. Help me to live with 'Heaven eyes' today, sharing Your hope with everyone I meet. I can't wait to see You face-to-face. Amen."

CONCLUSION

KEEP GROWING IN FAITH

Congratulations! You have officially reached the end of this book. We have traveled a long way together through these thirteen chapters. We started at the very beginning of time with **Creation**, explored the "Great Gap" caused by **Sin**, met our Hero and Savior, **Jesus**, and discovered how the **Holy Spirit** helps us walk through life every single day. We've looked at the importance of prayer, the beauty of the Church family, and the incredible promise of a New Home.

But here is a very important truth to hold onto: even though you have finished the last page of this workbook, you have not finished the story. In fact, you are just getting to the most exciting part!

Think of this book like a **training manual** for a deep-sea diver or a detailed map for a mountain explorer. Reading the manual is important because it teaches you how the equipment works and where the dangers might be. However, the real excitement doesn't start until the diver finally jumps into the sparkling blue ocean. The real fun begins when the explorer actually starts hiking up the trail, smelling the pine trees and seeing the view for themselves. This book was designed to give you the "tools" and the "map" you need, but the **adventure** of walking with God is something that happens out there, in your real life, every single day for the rest of your life.

The "Three-Legged Stool" of Growth

How do you keep your faith strong now that you've finished these lessons? Following Jesus is a bit like riding a bike or learning a new sport; if you stop practicing, you might feel a bit wobbly. To keep your faith from wobbling, it helps to focus on three main habits. Imagine a stool with three legs. If all three legs are strong, the stool is sturdy and you can sit on it safely. But if one leg is missing or broken, the stool will tip over. To keep your spiritual life sturdy, keep these three things in balance:

1. Keep Talking (Communication)

Don't let your conversation with God stop just because you finished the "Prayer" chapter. Remember, He is your Heavenly Father, and He never gets tired of hearing from you. Communication is the heartbeat of any relationship. If you stopped talking to your best friend, your friendship would eventually feel distant. It's the same with God. You don't need a formal "prayer closet" or a list of big words. Just talk to Him. Talk to Him about your breakfast, the math problem that is confusing you, and the things you are excited about for the weekend.

2. Keep Eating (The Bible)

Just like your physical body needs healthy food to grow taller and stronger, your spirit needs "God's Word" to stay healthy. The Bible is often called "Spiritual Milk" or "Bread." You don't have to read ten chapters a day to be a "good Christian." Instead, try to find one verse or one story each day. Read it slowly. Think about it while you brush your teeth. Ask the Holy Spirit, "God, what are You trying to tell me in this verse today?"

3. Keep Walking (Action)

Faith isn't just something we *know* in our heads; it's something we *do* with our lives. James, a writer in the Bible, said that faith without action is like a body without breath—it isn't really alive! When the Holy Spirit gives you a "nudge" to be kind to someone who is lonely, or to tell the truth even when it might get you in trouble, follow that nudge! Every time you choose God's way over your own way, your "faith muscles" get a little bit stronger.

Understanding the Seasons of Growth

In nature, trees don't grow at the exact same speed every single day. In the spring, they sprout beautiful green leaves and flowers. In the summer, they grow deep roots. In the autumn, they might lose their leaves, and in the winter, they look like they are sleeping. But even in the winter, the tree is still alive, and its roots are still there.

Your life with God will have seasons, too.

- **Spring Seasons:** Sometimes everything feels new and exciting. You feel very close to God, and reading the Bible feels easy and fun.

- **Winter Seasons:** Sometimes you might feel a little bored, or God might feel far away. You might have questions that are hard to answer, or you might go through a sad time.

The most important thing to remember is that **God is with you in every season.** Just because you don't "feel" like you are growing doesn't mean God has stopped working in you. Deep under the soil of your heart, He is still building your roots.

The Tool of Memory

One of the best ways to keep growing is to hide God's Word in your heart. In this book, we have looked at thirteen different **Focus Verses**. These aren't just sentences to read; they are like "Survival Gear" for your brain.

When you feel scared, you can remember: *"The Lord is my Shepherd."* When you feel like you aren't good enough, you can remember: *"By grace you have been saved."* When you feel alone, you can remember: *"I will never leave you."*

Activity: My Favorite Promise Look back through your favorite chapters. Choose one verse that you want to memorize so well that you could say it even if someone woke you up in the middle of the night. Write it in big, bold letters in the space below:

Activity: The "Growth Map" Reflection

Now that you've reached the end, it's helpful to look back at the trail you've climbed. Take a moment to think about these questions:

1. **What was the most surprising thing you learned about God's character?**

    ----

2. **Which "Home Lab" experiment helped you understand a spiritual truth the best? Why?**

    ----

3. **What is one thing you used to be confused about that feels clearer now?**

    ----

4. Who is one person you can share these truths with? (A sibling, a friend, or a cousin?)

The Golden Rule of the Journey: Grace Over Perfection

As you move forward, there is one very important thing you must never forget: **God is not looking for you to be perfect.** If you think that growing in faith means you never make a mistake again, you will end up feeling very frustrated. We are all "works in progress." Imagine a construction site for a beautiful skyscraper. Some days there are piles of dirt everywhere. Some days it looks messy and unfinished. But the Architect has the blueprints, and He knows exactly what the building will look like when it's done.

You are God's "construction site."

- There will be days when you make great choices and reflect His glory perfectly.
- There will be days when you lose your temper, tell a lie, or act selfishly.

When you mess up, the enemy (sin) wants you to hide from God, just like Adam and Eve did in the garden. But God wants you to do the opposite. He wants you to run **to** Him. Because of Chapter 8 (Grace), you can always say, "Father, I messed up. Please forgive me and help me try again."

God isn't a mean judge waiting for you to fail so He can punish you. He is a loving Father who is cheering for you as you learn to walk. When a baby is learning to walk and they trip and fall, the parents don't get angry, they pick the baby up, give them a hug, and encourage them to take another step. That is exactly how God feels about you.

Remember Chapter 10? You are part of a family. One of the biggest mistakes a Christian can make is trying to grow all by themselves. We are like the coals in the grill—we stay "on fire" when we are bunched together.

Make it a priority to stay connected to your church family.

- Listen to your teachers.

- Ask questions when you don't understand something.

- Find older Christians who can encourage you.

- Be a "helper" to younger kids who are just starting their journey.

When we walk together, the journey is much more fun and much less scary.

The Final Promise: He Finishes What He Starts

The Bible contains a beautiful promise in a book called Philippians. It says: *"He who began a good work in you will carry it on to completion until the day of Christ Jesus."*

This means that growing in faith isn't something you have to do all by yourself. God is the one who "began" the work in your heart. He is the one who gave you the desire to learn about Him. And He is the one who promises to "complete" it.

You don't have to worry if you are "strong enough" to stay a Christian for the rest of your life. You aren't holding onto God; He is holding onto you. And His grip is very, very strong.

The Adventure Awaits

You are a special creation. You have been rescued by the Savior. You are guided by the Holy Spirit. You are a child of the King. You have a home in Heaven.

Now, it's time to close this book and open your eyes to the world around you. Every person you meet is someone God loves. Every day you wake up is a chance to show His glory. Every challenge you face is a chance to trust His power.

Keep reading. Keep praying. Keep loving. The adventure is just beginning!

Talk to God

"Dear Heavenly Father, thank You for everything I have learned in these thirteen chapters. Thank You for being my Creator, my Shepherd, my Savior, and my King. As I finish this workbook, I ask that You would keep growing my faith every single day. Help me to remember Your promises when I am scared and Your grace when I make mistakes. Help me to be a light in this world and to show others how wonderful You are. I am so glad I belong to Your family. I love You, Lord. Amen."

APPENDIX A

THE ATTRIBUTES OF GOD

Imagine you have a pen pal. You have never met them in person, but they write you letters every week. In the letters, they tell you about themselves. They might say, *"I am tall,"* or *"I have red hair,"* or *"I am very good at math."* These descriptions are called **Attributes**. An attribute is simply a trait or a quality that makes a person who they are.

If you asked your best friend to list your attributes, they might say you are funny, fast, kind, or brown-eyed. But what if we asked the Bible to list **God's** attributes? What is God actually *like*?

Many people make the mistake of thinking God is just a "super-sized" version of a human. They think He is like a nice grandfather in the sky, or a superhero with a cape. But the Bible teaches us something very different. It teaches us **Theology Proper**, which is the study of God Himself. It tells us that God is not just "bigger" than us; He is a completely different kind of being. He is the Creator, and we are the creatures.

In this special section, we are going to explore **Ten Great Attributes of God**. Some of these are things God shares with us (like Love), and some are things that belong only to Him (like being All-Knowing).

Get ready to stretch your brain. These truths are huge. They are heavier than mountains and deeper than the ocean. But learning them is the most important thing you will ever do, because the more you know about who God is, the more you will trust Him, love Him, and worship Him.

1. God is Eternal (Infinite)

He has no beginning and no end.

Have you ever tried to think about "forever"? It hurts your brain a little bit, doesn't it? Everything we know in our world has a beginning and an end.

- You had a birthday (a beginning).
- Your shoes were made in a factory on a certain day.
- Even the sun and the stars had a moment when they were created.

But God is different. He is **Eternal**. This means He never had a birthday. There was never a time when God did not exist. Before the universe was made, before angels were created, and before time itself started ticking, God was there.

Imagine a long piece of string that represents time. It stretches from the past to the future. You are a tiny dot on that string. But God isn't on the string at all. He created the string! He stands outside of time. He sees the days of the dinosaurs, the day you were born, and the day looking 10,000 years into the future all at the same exact moment. He is the "Alpha and Omega," the Beginning and the End.

Why Does This Matter? Because God is Eternal, He is never in a rush. He is never "running out of time" to fix your problems. Also, because He has always existed, He is the only One who truly knows how the story of the world ends. You can trust Him with your future because He is already there!

> **The Verse:** "Before the mountains were born or you brought forth the whole world, from everlasting to everlasting you are God." (Psalm 90:2)

He never changes, grows, or improves.

Think about how much you have changed since you were a baby. You grew taller. You learned how to talk. You learned math. Maybe you used to like strained peas, but now you hate them. Humans are constantly changing. We change our minds, our moods, and our plans.

God is **Immutable**. That is a big theological word that means "He does not mutate" or change. God never grows "older." He never learns something new (because He already knows everything). He never gets stronger (because He is already all-powerful). And most importantly, He never changes His character.

God will never wake up on the "wrong side of the bed" and be grumpy with you. He will never decide that He doesn't love you anymore. He will never cancel a promise He made in the Bible. In a world where everything changes, your friends, your school, your feelings, God is like a giant, unmovable Rock. He is the same yesterday, today, and forever.

Why Does This Matter? If God changed, we couldn't trust Him. Imagine if God was kind on Monday but mean on Tuesday! You would be scared to pray. But because He is Immutable, you know exactly who He is every single time you talk to Him. You can build your life on Him because He will never shift under your feet.

The Verse: *"I the Lord do not change. So you, the descendants of Jacob, are not destroyed." (Malachi 3:6)*

3. God is Omnipresent (Everywhere)

He is present everywhere, all the time.

"Omni" is a Latin word that means "All." So, "Omnipresent" means "All-Present."

As a human, you can only be in one place at a time. If you are at school, you can't be at home. If you are in your bedroom, you can't be in the kitchen. But God is **Spirit**, which means He doesn't have a physical body that limits Him to one spot.

God is fully present in this room with you right now. But at this exact same second, He is fully present on the other side of the world in

Australia, and He is fully present on the moon, and He is fully present in a galaxy a billion light-years away. He isn't "stretched out" like a thin layer of butter over bread. He is *fully* everywhere.

This means you can never run away from God. In the Bible, a man named Jonah tried to run away on a boat, but God was there. David wrote that even if he made his bed in the deepest ocean, God would be there.

Why Does This Matter? For a person who is disobeying God, this is a scary thought—you can't hide! But for a child of God, this is the most comforting thought in the world. It means you are never alone.

- When you walk into a new classroom and feel scared... God is there.

- When you are lying in bed in the dark... God is there.

- When you feel lonely... God is right beside you.

  The Verse: *"Where can I go from Your Spirit? Where can I flee from Your presence?" (Psalm 139:7)*

4. God is Omniscient (All-Knowing)

He knows everything: past, present, and future.

How much do you know? You probably know your multiplication tables, the names of your friends, and the rules of your favorite video game. But do you know how many stars are in the sky? Do you know what your friend is thinking right now? Do you know what will happen next Tuesday? No, of course not.

God is **Omniscient**. He knows *everything* that can be known.

- **He knows the Universe:** He counts the stars and calls them all by name (Psalm 147:4).

- **He knows the Future:** He knows exactly what is going to happen a thousand years from now.

- **He knows YOU:** He knows how many hairs are on your head. He knows what you are going to say before you even open your mouth. He knows your secrets, your fears, and your dreams.

God never has to "learn" anything. He never Googles an answer. He never says, "Oops, I didn't see that coming!" He is the expert on everything.

Why Does This Matter? Sometimes we think we know better than God. We think, *"I want this toy right now!"* or *"I want to do things my way!"* But because God is Omniscient, He sees the whole picture. If He says "No" to something, it's because He knows something you don't. Trusting an All-Knowing God means believing that His plan is smarter than our plan.

> **The Verse:** *"Great is our Lord and mighty in power; his understanding has no limit." (Psalm 147:5)*

5. God is Omnipotent (All-Powerful)

He can do anything that fits with His character.

Think of the strongest thing you can imagine. A hurricane? A nuclear explosion? The gravity of a black hole? Compared to God, all of those things are weaker than a tiny candlelight.

God is **Omnipotent**. He has unlimited power.

- He spoke, and the universe appeared out of nothing.
- He holds the planets in orbit with just the "word of His power."
- He can split seas, heal the sick, raise the dead, and calm storms.

There is no rock too heavy for Him to lift. There is no problem too hard for Him to solve. Satan is not God's equal; Satan is a created being. God could stop Satan with a single breath if He wanted to.

However, there are things God *cannot* do. He cannot lie. He cannot sin. He cannot stop being God. This isn't because He is weak; it's because He is perfect. He cannot do anything that goes against His own good nature.

Why Does This Matter? When we face big problems—like sickness or scary news—we can feel small and helpless. But our Father is the Strongest Being in Existence. Praying to an Omnipotent God means knowing that He is able to handle whatever you give Him. As the angel told Mary, *"For nothing will be impossible with God."*

> **The Verse:** *"Ah, Sovereign Lord, you have made the heavens and the earth by your great power and outstretched arm. Nothing is too hard for you." (Jeremiah 32:17)*

He is perfect and totally separate from sin.

The word **Holy** is the only attribute of God that is repeated three times in a row in the Bible: *"Holy, Holy, Holy."* In Hebrew culture, repeating something meant it was incredibly important.

To be Holy means two things:

1. **Unique:** God is in a class by Himself. He is "set apart" from creation. It's like comparing a diamond to a pile of mud. The diamond is special, rare, and pure.
2. **Pure:** God has absolutely no darkness in Him. He never has a bad thought. He never makes a mistake. He is blindingly, perfectly good.

Imagine looking directly at the sun. It is so bright and powerful that it hurts your eyes. That is a little bit like God's holiness. In the Bible, when people saw a glimpse of God's holiness, they fell down on their faces because they realized how small and sinful they were in comparison.

Why Does This Matter? Because God is Holy, He cannot be friends with sin. This is the bad news: our sin separates us from Him. But this is also why the Cross is so amazing. Jesus (the Holy One) took our sin so that we could be made holy and come close to God again. God's holiness reminds us that we should treat Him with respect and awe, not like a buddy we can ignore.

The Verse: *"Holy, holy, holy is the Lord Almighty; the whole earth is full of his glory." (Isaiah 6:3)*

7. God is Sovereign (King)

He has absolute authority and control over everything.

Who is in charge of your life? Your parents? Your teachers? The President? While those people have some authority, God has **Ultimate Authority**.

Sovereignty means that God is the King of Kings. He sits on the throne of the universe, and nothing happens without His permission.

- The wind blows where He tells it to.
- Kings and rulers only rise to power because He allows it.

- Even the bad things that happen are under His control, and He can turn them around for good.

Think of a chess master playing a game. Even if his opponent makes a crazy move, the master knows exactly how to counter it to win the game. God is the ultimate Master. Even when the world looks chaotic, God is never panicked. He is always in control, working out His plan perfectly.

Why Does This Matter? The world can be a scary place. There are wars, sicknesses, and accidents. If no one was in charge, that would be terrifying. But because God is Sovereign, we can relax. We know that the One driving the bus is good, wise, and powerful. We don't have to worry about the future because the King is already there.

The Verse: *"The Lord has established his throne in heaven, and his kingdom rules over all." (Psalm 103:19)*

8. God is Just (Righteous)

He always does what is right and punishes evil.

Have you ever seen a bully get away with being mean and thought, *"That's not fair!"*? We all have a sense of justice inside us. We want good to be rewarded and bad to be punished. Where did we get that feeling? We got it from our Creator.

God is the Perfect Judge. He is **Just**. This means He never cheats. He never plays favorites. He never accepts a bribe. He always does exactly what is right.

This is a scary attribute because it means God cannot just "wink" at our sin. If a human judge let a criminal go free just because he felt like it, he would be a corrupt judge. Because God is a good Judge, He must punish sin. This is why the world has consequences for bad actions.

Why Does This Matter? If God wasn't Just, there would be no hope for the world. The bad guys would win. But because God is Just, we know that one day, He will fix everything. He will punish every evil deed and wipe away every tear. It also makes us thankful for Jesus. On the Cross, God's Justice and God's Love met. Jesus took the punishment (Justice) so we could have the forgiveness (Mercy). God remained Just, but He also became our Savior.

The Verse: *"He is the Rock, his works are perfect, and all his ways are just. A faithful God who does no wrong, upright and just is he." (Deuteronomy 32:4)*

9. God is Love (Benevolent)

He gives of Himself for the good of others.

This is probably the most famous attribute of God, but it is often misunderstood. When the Bible says **"God is Love,"** it doesn't mean God is a fuzzy feeling. It means that at His very core, God is a Giver.

Even before the world was created, the Father, the Son, and the Holy Spirit loved each other perfectly. God didn't create us because He was lonely. He created us because His love is so big that it bubbled over! He wanted to share His joy with us.

God's love is not like human love.

- **Human Love** often says: "I love you *because* you are cute, or smart, or nice to me."
- **God's Love (Agape)** says: "I love you *even though* you are sinful, messy, and broken."

God didn't wait for you to clean yourself up before He loved you. As Romans 5:8 says, *"While we were still sinners, Christ died for us."* His love is an action, not just an emotion.

Why Does This Matter? You might feel unlovable sometimes. You might think, *"If people knew what I did, they wouldn't like me."* But God knows everything (Omniscience) and He still loves you completely. You don't have to earn His love by being good, and you can't lose His love by making a mistake. You are secure in His love forever.

The Verse: *"And so we know and rely on the love God has for us. God is love. Whoever lives in love lives in God, and God in them." (1 John 4:16)*

10. God is Faithful (True)

He always keeps His promises and never lies.

Have you ever had a friend promise to come to your party, but then they didn't show up? It hurts when people break their word. Sometimes people lie on purpose, but sometimes they just forget, or something comes up that they can't control.

God is **Faithful**. He is the ultimate Truth-Teller.

1. **He Cannot Lie:** It is impossible for God to deceive you. If He says it in the Bible, it is true.

2. **He Cannot Fail:** Nothing can stop Him from keeping His promise. No traffic jam, no sickness, no enemy can prevent God from doing what He said He would do.

The Bible is full of thousands of promises. God promised Noah he would be safe in the Ark. He promised Abraham a son. He promised to send a Savior. And He kept every single one. Because He was faithful in the past, we know He will be faithful in the future.

Why Does This Matter? Life is full of uncertainty. We don't know what will happen tomorrow. But we have a Faithful God who has promised, *"I will never leave you nor forsake you."* When you feel shaky, you can hold onto His promises like a handle on a subway train. He will not let go.

The Verse: *"Know therefore that the Lord your God is God; he is the faithful God, keeping his covenant of love to a thousand generations." (Deuteronomy 7:9)*

Summary: The God Who Is All These Things

Now, here is the most amazing thought of all: **God is all of these things at the exact same time.**

- He is not *sometimes* Just and *sometimes* Loving. He is fully Just and fully Loving at the same moment.

- He is not *sometimes* Powerful and *sometimes* Gentle. He is Omnipotent and Merciful at the same moment.

This is the God we worship. He is the Infinite, Unchanging, Everywhere-Present, All-Knowing, All-Powerful, Holy, Sovereign, Just, Loving, and Faithful King.

When you pray tonight, don't just picture a small, friendly figure. Picture this majestic God who holds the universe in His hands, and remember the miracle: **He knows your name, and He calls you His child.**

APPENDIX B
THE NAMES AND TITLES OF JESUS

In our modern world, names are often just labels. Your parents might have named you "Liam" or "Sophia" just because they liked the sound of it, or maybe because it was a family name. But in Bible times, a name was much more than a label. A name was a **description**. It told people who you were, what you were like, or what destiny God had planned for you.

- **Jacob** meant "Deceiver" (and he was tricky!).
- **Abraham** meant "Father of Many Nations" (and he was!).
- **Moses** meant "Drawn Out" (because he was pulled from the river).

When we come to Jesus, we find something amazing: He doesn't just have one name. Throughout the Bible, Jesus is given dozens of titles and names. Why? Because He is so wonderful and so complex that one name simply isn't enough to describe Him!

If you looked at a giant diamond, you would have to turn it over and over to see how the light sparkles from different angles. That is what we are going to do in this section. We are going to look at **Ten Great Titles of Jesus**. Each title is like a different angle of the diamond, showing us a different part of His mission, His power, and His love.

This study is called **Christology**. It answers the most important question anyone will ever ask you: *"Who is Jesus?"* Is He just a good teacher? Is He just a nice man who lived a long time ago? Or is He something far, far greater? Let's find out.

1. Jesus (The Savior)

The Name Above All Names

Let's start with the name you know best: **Jesus**. It's the name we use when we pray, sing, and read the Gospels. But did you know this name wasn't an accident? God the Father picked it out specifically. Before Jesus was even born, an angel appeared to Joseph and said, *"You are to give him the name Jesus, because he will save his people from their sins"* (Matthew 1:21).

In Hebrew, the name is **Yeshua** (Joshua), which translates to **"The Lord Saves."** Think about that for a moment. Every time Mary called Him for dinner, *"Jesus!"*, she was literally saying, *"The Lord Saves!"* His very name was a promise of what He came to do.

Many people in history have tried to save the world.

- Generals try to save people with armies.
- Doctors try to save people with medicine.
- Politicians try to save people with laws. But none of them could save us from our biggest problem: **Sin**. Only Jesus could do that. He didn't come just to be a "Helper" or a "Coach." He came to be a **Rescuer**. Imagine a lifeguard diving into stormy water to pull a drowning person out. That is what the name Jesus means. He dove into our messy world to pull us out of death.

Why Does This Matter? This name reminds us that we cannot save ourselves. If we could be "good enough" to get to heaven, we wouldn't need a Savior. The name Jesus keeps us humble, but it also gives us hope. No matter how big your mess is, His name is bigger. He is the Savior, not just the "Advisor."

2. Christ (The Anointed One)

The King God Promised

Many people think "Christ" is Jesus' last name, like "Smith" or "Johnson." But Christ isn't a name; it is a **Title**. It comes from the Greek word *Christos*, which translates the Hebrew word **Messiah**. Both words mean the same thing: **"The Anointed One."**

In the Old Testament, you didn't just get a crown when you became King; you got **anointed**. A prophet would take a horn filled with special, sweet-smelling oil and pour it over your head. This symbolized that God's Spirit was coming upon you to give you power and authority for a special job.

For thousands of years, the Jewish people waited for "The Messiah"—the Ultimate King who would be anointed not just with oil, but with the Spirit of God without limit. They waited and waited. When Peter finally said to Jesus, *"You are the Christ,"* he was saying, *"You are the One we have been waiting for! You are the true King!"*

Jesus holds three "Anointed" offices perfectly:

1. **Prophet:** He speaks God's words to us.
2. **Priest:** He connects us to God.
3. **King:** He rules over the world.

Why Does This Matter? Calling Him "Christ" means we are pledging allegiance to Him. It means we acknowledge that He is the Boss. We don't just admire Him; we obey Him. When you say "Jesus Christ," you are saying, "Jesus is my King."

3. The Word (The Logos)

God Speaking to Us

The Gospel of John starts with a very mysterious sentence: *"In the beginning was the Word, and the Word was with God, and the Word was*

God." Later, it says, *"The Word became flesh and made his dwelling among us."*

Who is "The Word"? It is Jesus! The Greek word used here is **Logos**. In ancient times, this word meant the "logic" or "reason" behind the universe. But John used it to mean something even more personal.

Think about what your words do. Your words take the invisible thoughts inside your head and make them audible so other people can understand them. If you don't speak, I can't know you.

- Jesus is **God's Voice**.
- God the Father is invisible; no one has ever seen Him. But Jesus is the "Word" that makes the invisible God visible.

If you want to know what God thinks, look at Jesus. If you want to know what God loves, look at Jesus. If you want to know how God feels about sin, look at Jesus. He is the perfect "explanation" of who God is. He is God speaking to humanity in a language we can finally understand: a human life.

Why Does This Matter? Sometimes we look at the sky and wonder, *"God, who are You? Are You angry? Are You far away?"* We don't have to guess! We have "The Word." Jesus shows us exactly who the Father is. If you have seen Jesus, you have seen the Father. He is the communication of God's heart to yours.

> **The Verse:** *"The Word became flesh and made his dwelling among us. We have seen his glory, the glory of the one and only Son." (John 1:14)*

4. The Lamb of God

The Perfect Sacrifice

This is one of the most tender, yet powerful titles of Jesus. When John the Baptist first saw Jesus coming toward him, he didn't shout, "Look! The Lion!" or "Look! The King!" He pointed and said, *"Look, the Lamb of God, who takes away the sin of the world!"*

To a modern kid, calling a strong man a "lamb" might sound like an insult. Lambs are fluffy, weak, and gentle. But to a Jewish person in Bible times, this title meant one thing: **Sacrifice**.

In the Old Testament, when someone sinned, they had to bring a lamb to the temple. The lamb had to be perfect, no spots, no sickness. The lamb would take the punishment for the person's sin. This happened millions of times over hundreds of years. But the blood of animal lambs couldn't truly wash away human sin; it was just a temporary covering. It was pointing forward to something better.

Jesus is the **Ultimate Lamb**.

- He lived a perfect life (no spots of sin).
- He went to the Cross willingly (silent like a lamb).
- He took the punishment for the *whole world*.

Because Jesus died as the Lamb, we don't have to sacrifice animals anymore. The price has been paid in full, once and for all.

Why Does This Matter? This title reminds us of how much our salvation cost. It wasn't free for Jesus. He had to lay down His life. It also reminds us that He is gentle. He didn't come to crush us; He came to die for us. When you feel guilty for something you did, remember the Lamb of God has already carried that sin away.

> **The Verse:** *"Worthy is the Lamb, who was slain, to receive power and wealth and wisdom and strength!" (Revelation 5:12)*

5. The Great High Priest

The Bridge Builder

In the Old Testament, the High Priest was a very important person. He was the only one allowed to go into the "Holy of Holies", the most special room in the temple where God's presence lived. Once a year, he would go in to represent the people to God. He was like a bridge between a Holy God and sinful people.

But human priests had problems.

1. They were sinful themselves, so they had to offer sacrifices for their own mistakes.
2. They eventually died, so you always needed a new one.

Jesus is our **Great High Priest**.

- **He is Sinless:** He doesn't need to apologize for Himself.
- **He is Eternal:** He never dies, so He is *always* there to represent us.
- **He is the Bridge:** He didn't just go into a temple made of stone; He went into Heaven itself!

Right now, at this very moment, Jesus is sitting next to God the Father. Do you know what He is doing? He is **Interceding** for you. That means He is talking to the Father on your behalf. When you pray, Jesus says, *"Father, hear them. They are with Me."* He is our advocate, our lawyer, and our representative.

Why Does This Matter? Sometimes we feel too ashamed to pray. We think, *"God doesn't want to hear from me."* But because Jesus is our High Priest, we can walk boldly into God's presence! We don't need a human priest or a special building to talk to God. We have a direct line through Jesus.

> **The Verse:** *"Therefore he is able to save completely those who come to God through him, because he always lives to intercede for them." (Hebrews 7:25)*

6. The Alpha and Omega

The Beginning and The End

Alpha is the first letter of the Greek alphabet (like "A"). Omega is the last letter of the Greek alphabet (like "Z").

When Jesus calls Himself the **Alpha and Omega**, He is saying, *"I am the A and the Z, and every letter in between."* This is a title of **Authority** and **Eternity**.

- **He was there at the start:** Jesus wasn't created in the manger in Bethlehem. He was there when the universe was spoken into existence (Colossians 1:16). He is the Author of life.
- **He will be there at the finish:** When history ends, Jesus will be the one standing there. He is the Finisher of our faith.

Think of your life like a book. Jesus wrote the first sentence (He gave you life), and He will write the last sentence (He will welcome you home). He surrounds you completely. You are never outside of His care because He exists before your problems start and after your problems end.

Why Does This Matter? This gives us incredible peace. If Jesus is the Alpha, it means He started a good work in you. If He is the Omega, it means He will finish it. He isn't a quitter. He oversees all of history, from the dinosaurs to the space age to the end of time. Nothing catches Him by surprise.

The Verse: *"I am the Alpha and the Omega, the First and the Last, the Beginning and the End." (Revelation 22:13)*

7. The Good Shepherd

The Protector and Guide

In ancient Israel, being a shepherd wasn't a relaxing job where you sat in the grass and played the flute. It was dangerous, dirty, hard work. Shepherds had to fight off lions, bears, and wolves. They had to sleep in the cold to watch over the sheep. They had to guide the sheep to water in the desert.

Sheep are not very smart animals. They get lost easily. They can't defend themselves (they have no claws or sharp teeth). They are totally dependent on the shepherd.

Jesus said, **"I am the Good Shepherd."** He contrasted Himself with a "hired hand." A hired worker runs away when the wolf comes because he doesn't own the sheep; he just wants the paycheck. But the Good Shepherd stays. He fights for the sheep. Jesus said He would even *lay down His life* for the sheep.

As our Shepherd, Jesus does three things:

1. **Feeds Us:** He gives us His Word.
2. **Leads Us:** He guides us through life by His Spirit.
3. **Finds Us:** When we wander off into sin, He comes looking for us. He doesn't wait for us to come back; He chases us down with His love.

Why Does This Matter? We all get lost. We all make bad decisions. It is comforting to know that we have a Shepherd who is committed to keeping us safe. When you feel lonely or confused about what decision to make, you can pray, *"Shepherd, lead me."* He knows the way to green pastures.

The Verse: *"I am the good shepherd. The good shepherd lays down his life for the sheep." (John 10:11)*

The One Who Chases Away Darkness

Imagine being in a cave, deep underground. It is pitch black. You can't see your hand in front of your face. You are terrified of falling into a hole or running into a rock. Then, suddenly, someone turns on a massive, bright flashlight. Instantly, everything changes. The fear goes away. You can see the path. You can see the danger.

Jesus said, **"I am the Light of the World."**

Our world can be a dark place. There is the darkness of **Sin** (people doing bad things). There is the darkness of **Ignorance** (people not knowing who God is). There is the darkness of **Hopelessness** (sadness and despair).

Jesus comes like a sunrise.

- He reveals the truth (so we don't stumble).
- He exposes sin (so we can clean it up).
- He brings warmth (healing our hearts).

Light has a very special property: **Darkness cannot defeat it.** You cannot shovel darkness into a room to get rid of the light. But you *can* bring a single candle into a dark room, and the darkness must flee. Jesus is the unconquerable Light.

Why Does This Matter? When you are confused or sad, you are in a "dark" place. Jesus promises that if you follow Him, you will *"never walk in darkness, but will have the light of life."* You don't have to stumble through life guessing what the meaning of everything is. Follow the Light, and you will see clearly.

> **The Verse:** *"I am the light of the world. Whoever follows me will never walk in darkness, but will have the light of life."* (John 8:12)

The One Who Satisfies

The Deep Dive Everybody gets hungry. You can eat the biggest Thanksgiving dinner in the world, but give it five or six hours, and your stomach will growl again. Physical food keeps us alive, but it never satisfies us permanently.

Jesus used this fact to teach a huge lesson. After He miraculously fed 5,000 people with lunch, they wanted to make Him King just so He would keep giving them free food. Jesus told them, *"Do not work for food that spoils... I am the Bread of Life."*

He was saying that human souls have a "hunger," too. We are hungry for love, for meaning, and for purpose. People try to fill that hunger with all kinds of "junk food":

- Video games
- Popularity
- Money
- Success

But none of those things fill the empty spot inside. We always want more. Jesus is the only "food" that fills the hole in our hearts. When we know Him, our soul says, *"Ah, this is what I was missing."* He gives us life that lasts forever.

Why Does This Matter? Are you ever bored, even when you have lots of toys? Are you ever lonely, even when you are with friends? That is "soul hunger." It's your heart telling you that you need Jesus. Run to Him, and He will satisfy you in a way that nothing else can.

The Verse: *"Then Jesus declared, 'I am the bread of life. Whoever comes to me will never go hungry.'"* (John 6:35)

10. The King of Kings and Lord of Lords

The Final Victor

We end with the most majestic title of all. When Jesus came the first time, He was a humble baby in a manger. He was a suffering servant. He allowed men to arrest Him and kill Him.

But the Bible tells us that when Jesus comes *back*, He will look very different. The book of Revelation describes Him riding a white horse, with eyes like blazing fire and many crowns on His head. On His robe is written the name: **King of Kings and Lord of Lords**.

This is a title of **Absolute Supremacy**.

- There are many "kings" (presidents, rulers, authorities) on earth. Jesus is the King *over* them.

- There are many "lords" (bosses, leaders). Jesus is the Lord *over* them.

He isn't just a religious leader; He is the Ruler of the Cosmos. One day, every knee will bow and every tongue will confess that He is Lord. The baby in the manger is actually the CEO of the Universe.

Why Does This Matter? Sometimes it looks like the bad guys are winning. It looks like Jesus is weak or that people have forgotten Him. This title reminds us of the truth: Jesus is currently seated on the Throne. He has already won the war against sin and death. We are on the winning team! We can live with courage because our Big Brother is the King of everything.

> **The Verse:** *"On his robe and on his thigh he has this name written: King of kings and Lord of lords." (Revelation 19:16)*

APPENDIX C

THE ESSENTIALS OF TRUTH
(THE APOSTLES' CREED)

Have you ever seen a massive ship docked at a harbor? Even when the waves get choppy and the wind starts to howl, that giant ship doesn't float away. Why? Because it is held in place by a massive, heavy iron **anchor** that goes deep under the water and hooks into the solid ground.

As a Christian, your "ship" is your life, and the "ocean" is the world around you. Sometimes the world gets very confusing. You might hear different people saying different things about God. One person might say, *"God is just a force in nature,"* while another says, *"It doesn't matter what you believe as long as you are nice."* How do you know what the truth is? You need an anchor. For almost 2,000 years, Christians have used something called **The Apostles' Creed** as their anchor.

What is a "Creed"? The word "Creed" comes from the Latin word *Credo*, which simply means **"I believe."** A creed is a short summary of the most important "must-know" truths of the Bible. It isn't a replacement for the Bible, but it's like a "Cheat Sheet" that helps you remember the most important parts.

The Apostles' Creed is the oldest and most famous summary of the Christian faith. It is called the "Apostles'" creed not because the 12 apostles wrote it themselves, but because it contains the exact teaching that the apostles taught. It is divided into 12 "articles" or points. In this section, we are going to walk through each point like a detective, unlocking the **Systematic Theology** behind each sentence.

The Apostles' Creed

I believe in God, the Father almighty, creator of heaven and earth. I believe in Jesus Christ, his only Son, our Lord, who was conceived by the Holy Spirit and born of the virgin Mary. He suffered under Pontius Pilate, was crucified, died, and was buried; he descended to hell. The third day he rose again from the dead. He ascended to heaven and is seated at the right hand of God the Father almighty. From there he will come to judge the living and the dead. I believe in the Holy Spirit, the holy catholic church, the communion of saints, the forgiveness of sins, the resurrection of the body, and the life everlasting. Amen.

Article 1: "I believe in God, the Father almighty, creator of heaven and earth."

The Deep Dive (Theology Proper) We start with the most basic truth: God exists. But the Creed doesn't just say "God"; it calls Him **Father Almighty**. This tells us two things about His character.

1. **Father:** He is personal and loving. He isn't a cold "energy" in space. He is a Dad who cares for His children.
2. **Almighty:** He has all the power (*Omnipotence*).

The Creed also confirms that God is the **Creator**. This means the world isn't an accident. Every mountain, every molecule, and every galaxy was designed by Him. Because He made it, He owns it.

Workbook Challenge: Detective Work Look up **Genesis 1:1** and **Psalm 103:13**.

- Genesis 1:1 tells us God is: ______________________________

  ____

- Psalm 103:13 tells us God is a: ______________________________

  ____

Think About It: If God is both your *Father* (Loving) and *Almighty* (Powerful), why should you never have to be afraid?

Article 2: "I believe in Jesus Christ, his only Son, our Lord..."

The Deep Dive (Christology) Now we move to the second person of the Trinity: Jesus. The Creed uses three specific titles here that define our **Christology**.

- **Jesus Christ:** As we learned in Appendix B, this means "The Savior" and "The Anointed King."

- **His Only Son:** This tells us that Jesus is the same "stuff" as God. Just like a baby puppy is a dog because its parents are dogs, Jesus is God because He is the Son of God. He is "One" with the Father.

- **Our Lord:** This means He is our Master. We don't just ask Him for help; we follow His orders.

Check for Understanding: If Jesus is the "Only Son," can there be other ways to get to God? (Circle one) **YES / NO**

Why? ____

____

Article 3: "...who was conceived by the Holy Spirit and born of the virgin Mary."

The Deep Dive (The Incarnation) This is one of the most mysterious parts of our faith. It describes the **Incarnation**—when God became a human.

- **Conceived by the Holy Spirit:** This means Jesus didn't have a human father. He is fully God.

- **Born of the Virgin Mary:** This means He was a real human baby who was born just like you. He is fully Man.

Jesus is the **God-Man**. He had to be a man so He could represent us and die in our place. He had to be God so His life would be worth enough to pay for *everyone's* sins.

Workbook Activity: The Two Natures of Jesus List two things Jesus did that showed He was **Human** and two things that showed He was **God**.

- Human: ____
- God: ____
- Human: ____
- God: ____

Article 4: "He suffered under Pontius Pilate, was crucified, died, and was buried..."

The Deep Dive (Atonement) The Creed mentions a real historical person: **Pontius Pilate**. He was the Roman governor. This is important because it reminds us that Jesus' death wasn't a fairy tale or a myth. It happened at a specific time, in a specific place, in front of witnesses.

Crucified, died, and was buried: This proves that Jesus really died. He didn't just faint or fall into a deep sleep. He went into the ground. He gave up His life completely to pay our "Sin Debt." This is called **Substitutionary Atonement**—He stood in our place.

Think About It: Why do you think the Creed mentions that Jesus was *buried?* ____

____

(Hint: It's to show that His death was 100% real. You don't bury someone who is still breathing!)

Article 5: "...he descended to hell. The third day he rose again from the dead."

The Deep Dive (The Resurrection) The phrase "descended to hell" can be confusing. It doesn't mean Jesus went to be punished by the devil. In the original language, it means He went to the "place of the dead" (Hades/Sheol). It means He experienced death to the very fullest.

But then comes the best part: **The third day He rose again.** This is the **Resurrection**.

- If Jesus stayed dead, He would just be a dead hero.
- Because He rose, He is a **Living King**.

The Resurrection is the "receipt" that proves God accepted Jesus' payment for our sins. It shows that Jesus is stronger than death and stronger than the grave.

Workbook Quiz: True or False?

1. Jesus rose from the dead only in spirit, not in His body. **T / F**
2. Jesus rose on the third day, just like He promised. **T / F**
3. The resurrection means death is defeated forever. **T / F**

Article 6: "He ascended to heaven and is seated at the right hand of God the Father almighty."

The Deep Dive (The Ascension) After spending 40 days with His friends after the Resurrection, Jesus went back up to Heaven. This is called the **Ascension**.

He is currently **seated at the right hand of God**. In the ancient world, the "right hand" was the place of highest honor and power. Imagine a king's throne room; the person at his right hand is the one who carries out all his plans. Jesus isn't just "resting" in Heaven; He is **Ruling**. He is governing the universe and listening to our prayers.

Faith at Work: How does it make you feel to know that your Savior is currently sitting in the highest place of power in the universe?

Article 7: "From there he will come to judge the living and the dead."

The Deep Dive (Eschatology) This part of Systematic Theology is called **Eschatology**—the study of last things. The Creed promises that history is going somewhere. Jesus is coming back!

When He returns, He will be the **Judge**. This sounds scary, but for a Christian, it is actually good news. It means that one day, all the bullying, all the lying, and all the unfair things in the world will be dealt with. Jesus will set everything right.

Think About It: If you are "in Christ" (covered by His grace), do you have to be afraid of the Judge? (Check one)

[ ] Yes, I'm still scared.

[ ] No, because my Judge is also my Savior who died for me.

Article 8: "I believe in the Holy Spirit..."

The Deep Dive (Pneumatology) This is **Pneumatology**—the study of the Spirit. The Creed doesn't say "I believe in a good feeling" or "I believe in an invisible force." It says, "I believe in the Holy Spirit."

The Holy Spirit is the third Person of the Trinity. He is just as much God as the Father and the Son. As we learned in Chapter 9, He is our Helper, our Teacher, and our Comforter. He is the one who lives inside us to help us say "No" to sin and "Yes" to God.

Fill in the Blank: In John 14:26, Jesus calls the Holy Spirit the

----

Article 9: "...the holy catholic church, the communion of saints..."

The Deep Dive (Ecclesiology) This article is about **Ecclesiology**—the study of the Church. You might see the word "catholic" and think it refers only to the Roman Catholic Church, but that isn't what it means here. The word "catholic" (with a small 'c') simply means **"Universal."** It means the Church is one giant family that includes every true believer in every country and every time period.

- **The Communion of Saints:** This means we are all connected. We share the same Father, the same Spirit, and the same Hope. We are never alone!

Workbook Activity: My Church Family List three things you can do to help the "Communion of Saints" in your own town.

1. ____

2. ____

3. ____

Article 10: "...the forgiveness of sins..."

The Deep Dive (Hamartiology & Soteriology) This is the heart of the Gospel! **Hamartiology** is the study of sin (the problem), and **Soteriology** is the study of salvation (the solution).

Because of what Jesus did on the Cross, our sins are not just "hidden"—they are **Forgiven**. This means God takes our "record" of bad things and wipes it completely clean. He doesn't hold our past against us. When we come to Him in faith, He sees us as "Justified" (Just-as-if-I'd never sinned).

Think About It: Imagine you had a chalkboard covered in 1,000 mistakes. Then, someone comes with a wet sponge and wipes it so clean that the board looks brand new.

- Who is the one with the sponge?

- How does it feel to know your board is clean?

Article 11: "...the resurrection of the body..."

The Deep Dive (Glorification) Some people think that when we die, we just become "ghosts" forever. But the Bible teaches something much more exciting: **The Resurrection of the Body**.

Just as Jesus rose from the dead in a real, physical body, one day He will raise us, too! Our "new" bodies will be like our old ones, but better.

- No more glasses.
- No more braces.
- No more wheelchairs.
- No more getting tired or sick.

God loves His creation so much that He isn't just going to save our "souls"—He is going to save our **bodies**, too.

Workbook Activity: Imagine Your New Body If you could describe your "Resurrection Body" in three words, what would they be?

1. ____

2. ____

3. ____

Article 12: "...and the life everlasting. Amen."

The Deep Dive (Eternal Life) The Creed ends where everything begins: **Everlasting Life**. This isn't just about living forever (everyone exists forever somewhere); it's about **Life with God**.

Eternal life starts the moment you trust Jesus, and it continues forever in the New Heaven and the New Earth. It is a life of joy, discovery, and friendship with the King of the Universe.

Amen: We end the Creed with "Amen." This isn't just a way to say "The End." It is a Hebrew word that means **"So be it"** or **"It is true!"** It's like putting a period at the end of a sentence or a seal on a letter. You are saying, *"I stake my life on these truths."*

Summary: Your Faith Foundation

You have just walked through the 12 pillars of Christian Theology! Whenever you feel confused or when someone tells you something about God that doesn't sound quite right, come back to the Creed.

- Is God the Father? **Yes.**
- Is Jesus the Son who died and rose? **Yes.**
- Is the Holy Spirit our Helper? **Yes.**
- Is there forgiveness and eternal life? **Yes!**

If you hold onto these 12 truths, your anchor will stay deep in the ground, and your ship will stay safe, no matter how big the waves get.

Workbook Final Check: Go back and read the entire Apostles' Creed out loud. As you read each line, think about the "Deep Dive" we just did.

Which of the 12 articles is most comforting to you today?

____

____

____

Why?

HERE'S ANOTHER BOOK BY JAMES NORTHWELL THAT YOU MIGHT LIKE